Desperate Christian parents and teachers may .... yet use methods of behaviour modification tha. .... of the gospel. Can the spiritual core of Christian nurture yield practical insights? Dr. Sisemore, a believing Bible scholar and psychologist, shows that it must. His approach is what the Bible calls wisdom. His book is as rich in Biblical instruction as it is in psychological insight.

The Late Edmund P. Clowney
Emeritus Professor of Practical Theology
Westminster Seminary, Escondido California

In our increasingly dysfunctional society, parents – including many Christian parents – are searching for guiding principles which will give stability, security and wholesome direction to family life. What we all need is wisdom, faith and courage. In these pages Timothy Sisemore has gone a long way to meet our needs. Here is a straightforward, readable, challenging and practical manual – just what parents are looking for.

Sinclair B. Ferguson
Senior Pastor, First Presbyterian Church, Columbia, South Carolina

With growing confusion over how to bring up children in the home, how to cater for their needs in the church and how to relate them to the sacraments, Christians are desperately in need of constructive help in the realm of nurturing children. Such help is precisely what Dr. Sisemore has provided in this significant and accessible work. Starting with a biblically grounded basis for the way in which we are to regard children, he goes on to develop the most helpful of principles which he then applies to the task of child-rearing in the home and in the church. Anyone who has any true concern for the spiritual welfare of children in the present age must read this book!

Mark G. Johnston
Grove Chapel, London

Tim Sisemore is to be commended for this book. It is timely, biblically, theologically, and philosophically sound. From that framework he has written a solidly practical book that I commend to parents, grandparents, and others who have responsibilities with today's children. The author is very candid and open to make no promises to parents that God does not make, like so many other books tend to do e.g. if you do 'a' then 'b' will happen. The book underscores the need not only to teach our children about God but also to develop a worldview that enables them to see the totality of their Christian faith in all things.

The author convinces me that he understands our time and what the Lord would have us to do. We and our children must know the Lord and his Word, but we must also know the world and how to evaluate things in light of that knowledge. This book will serve a real purpose in driving home that point. We cannot isolate nor truly insulate our children from the world but we can equip them to live Christianly in this world. Sisemore is clear on that point and I commend him for that emphasis. His suggestions on procedures for those things are helpful, realistic, and definitely applicable, particularly in emphasizing the need to teach our children to think and to think strategically about life and reality. I am pleased not only to endorse this book but will recommend it as an important book for the intended family and church audience.

Charles Dunahoo
Coordinator of Christian Education and Publications
for the Presbyterian Church in America

The last section—on "the nurture of children in the church"—is worth the price of the book. Dr. Sisemore addresses a need that's crucial for parents and church leaders today. He alerts us to see, enfold and spiritually cultivate our covenant children with fresh vitality driven by biblical teaching and Reformed doctrine. At every turn in this book, you will find a consistent God-ward focus accented with practical, hands-on guidance.

Rev. Thomas R. Patete,
Executive Director, Great Commission Publications

OUR COVENANT WITH KIDS

Biblical Nurture in Home and Church

TIMOTHY A. SISEMORE

CHRISTIAN
FOCUS

Timothy A. Sisemore earned his doctorate in clinical psychology from Fuller Theological Seminary in Pasadena, California, where he also earned the M.A. in Theology. He currently is Academic Dean and Associate Professor of Counseling at the Psychological Studies Institute in Atlanta and Chattanooga, and maintains a clinical practice at the Chattanooga Bible Institute Counseling Center. He is married to Ruth and they have one daughter, Erin.

© Timothy Sisemore

ISBN 978-1-84550-350-5

10 9 8 7 6 5 4 3 2 1

Published in 2000 with the title
Of Such is the Kingdom
Reprinted 2998
by
Christian Focus Publications
Geanies House, Fearn, Ross-shire
IV20 1TW, Great Britain

Cover design by Paul Lewis
Printed by CPD, Wales

CONTENTS

To my parents

Who have blessed many children
with the 'book' of their lives

1

CHRISTIAN PARENTING
IN A HOSTILE WORLD

*'Doctrine is the foundation of duty; if the theory is not correct,
the practice cannot be right. Tell me what a man believes, and
I will tell you what he will do.'* (Tryon Edwards).

Frankly, I am glad I am not a child. Oh, don't get me wrong;
I enjoyed my childhood. I carry fond memories of carefree
times, waking up with the feeling of freedom and anticipation
as I knew play was my only agenda that day. I went to a public
school where the Bible was taught and most of the children
claimed to be Christians. By my teenage years, I was aware that
some students were involved in drugs and sex, but these were
the 'oddballs', a group apart from the mainstream of students
who were basically moral. I enjoyed television, movies and music,
but most of the entertainment was fairly innocent by today's
standards. There seemed to be a conspiracy to promote good
values wherever I looked, be it at home, school, church, or the
media. Children were largely protected from the immoral trends
that were building up momentum in the adult world.

Times have changed. As a Christian psychologist who interviews
children and youths for a living, I am struck by the changes
almost daily. For many children, getting an education at school

is a goal secondary to protecting themselves from violence. Being 'good' is something that will likely bring ridicule from peers who exert pressure toward experimentation with alcohol, drugs, sex, truancy and deceit. The media has found a wonderful market in children and teens, and exploits their sinful desires to sell products, cleverly managing to wrangle money from the hands of disapproving parents. Yet many parents are not so disapproving. These actually promote the cultural rejection of moral values or at least remain quiet on the issue in order to protect the self-esteem of their children from those who might harm it by correcting their behaviour. I am embarrassed to say that fellow psychologists are largely to blame for paralysing parents' moral impulses by (falsely) warning them that responding negatively to the behaviour of their children will strip them of good feelings about themselves.

These changes have not been lost on the followers of Christ. Christians have led the battle-cry against immoral cultural trends that threaten our children. We loudly protest against abortions that deprive children of the chance to live and grow. We discourage our offspring from listening to the cruder forms of contemporary music and try to replace it with Christian music that often sounds much the same. We preach abstinence until marriage and limit young children's exposure to the increasingly graphic sexuality beamed by television into our homes.

Christians have developed strong organizations, such as James Dobson's 'Focus on the Family', which are explicitly designed to promote what we often call 'family values'. As state-run schools have rendered God irrelevant to their agendas, believers have founded numerous Christian schools to ensure that their children see God as part of all of life. Some parents take matters more directly into their hands and school their children at home. Churches reach out to young people, offering entertaining activities to lure them off the streets and to give opportunity to speak to them of Christ. Children are given special attention in many church services through 'children's sermons' or are provided their own worship opportunity in a separate 'children's church' where the lesson is more on their level.

One of the major Christian strategies for combating the negative influences of our day is the written word. Books and magazines flood the market with advice for maintaining (or regaining) control over children and pointing them to Christ. Concerned parents, anxious to protect their progeny, make many of these bestsellers. It would appear the person concerned about the children under his or her care has sufficient resources for the task. This brings us to a crucial question that must be answered before proceeding with the present contribution to the Christian parenting literature: Why do we need another book on the subject?

My answer is, for all our efforts to reach our children, we are failing. Children of Christian parents, according to many surveys, don't act very differently to those of unbelievers when it comes to many of the moral issues of our day. Many profess Christ, but only with a frail faith that is easily bullied by the influence of the world. The faith that we are passing on is not the hearty faith of the gospel that can stand against the evil forces of our day. Many of our children believe in God, but fail to see how all of life is to be lived to his glory. They take on the shallow view of Christianity that provides 'fire insurance' for the afterlife but is too weak to move them to serious commitment.

I believe I know why we are failing. Our feelings for our children appear to be intact, and our eagerness to reach them cannot be challenged. However, I fear in our zeal to protect them and keep them from evil we have misunderstood the threats to our children and have offered shallow solutions to very deep problems. We fret and fuss in concern, then grab 'how to' answers to the problems as we perceive them, only to find they are inadequate. We have misjudged the severity of the threat, and offered grossly inadequate responses as a result.

How firm is our foundation?

A closer look at most Christian books on parenting will show a variety of theories on how to bring up children at the dawn of the new millennium. Many, frankly, are what I call 'baptized psychology'. The author takes a favourite psychological theory, searches the Scriptures for some verses to support it, and offers it to parents. Others are less well informed, being merely personal opinions dressed up with clever stories and an entertaining presentation to encourage parents, but fail to offer serious solutions. Some are more biblical, taking key references and building practical suggestions from them. What is missing in all of this is an effort to examine all that the Bible says about children, place it into a comprehensive framework, and use this as a foundation upon which to build our ministry to children. It will take a full-orbed biblical worldview about children to equip us for victory. Sadly, this need comes at a time when many Christians don't like to think deeply about their faith in any area, shunning 'theology' or anything more demanding than simple, practical suggestions.

The frog in the kettle

The neglect of well-reasoned, biblical thinking about children is rendered more scandalous given the major changes taking place behind the scenes in the world around us. While Christians are alert to obvious assaults on our beliefs, we blindly follow the culture in ways we do not realize. This is in part due to our accepting the contemporary stress on experience over absolute truth, with little consideration of the implications. Stimulation, not reflection, is valued, and we are easily caught up in this error. But to overlook such important changes in the 'philosophy' of the world is to enhance the risk of losing our children to it. Ignorance of these trends will expose us to the fate of the frog in the kettle whose demise was due to its lack of awareness of the slowly changing conditions of its environment. Christians easily miss several critical themes, and an awareness of these will help us grasp the importance of thinking more deeply about our ministry to children.

THE LOSS OF TRUTH

Throughout most of history, people believed in the idea of truth. Seeking truth was the motive for philosophy and science. This pursuit was driven by the belief that absolute truth existed and that anything short of that was insufficient. People believed that we would reach truth through the power of human reason that would develop great sciences and technology and so solve the world's problems. This experiment has failed. The products of man's reason have not led to truth. The same nuclear physics that keeps people warm with electricity supplies the technology for weapons that can destroy entire populations. Education was to solve the problems of the human race as we believed greater knowledge (bringing us closer to 'truth') would eliminate the central problem of ignorance. Yet, crime and poverty increased none the less. The notion that sexually educating our children in schools would lead to a reduction of pregnancies and venereal diseases has proved to be grossly inaccurate.

Modern thinkers, distraught by the failure of the pursuit of truth, have given up the search, concluding that objective truth does not exist. Enter the postmodern ideas of making one's own truth and rewriting historical 'facts' to match current values. Since there is no truth, every idea has equal value and contradictions can be ignored. New age spirituality thus draws from various religious traditions to find experiences that the individual might seek, disrespecting the belief systems from which they originate.

Christians often fail to see that this is the backdrop of our modern disregard for doctrine. We say, 'Just give me Jesus', but avoid any doctrinal statements that might actually define who he is. We seek the benefits that the Christian faith might bring us, but refuse to see it as a system of doctrine, or truth.

An example of how relativism has impacted the followers of Christ can be seen in a recent survey of Americans where three quarters of the population denied believing in absolute truth. Amazingly, 62% of evangelical Christians agreed,[1] suggesting that the majority of people who believe in the Bible and in Jesus Christ as the Way, the Truth, and the Life, do not believe in absolute truth! This strains our sense of logic. Yet, it can be explained by saying that, for some people, Jesus is the truth for them, but not the Truth in an absolute sense. The value of the Christian faith is, then, in its meaning for particular individuals. We downplay doctrine because it assumes a particular thing is true apart from our individual experience, and thus sets us in opposition to the thinking of the world.

This is seen in a larger scale in churches where programmes are designed to be 'seeker sensitive' by providing uplifting experiences and entertainment. Doctrinal issues again are avoided because they might discourage numerical growth, the primary goal of many churches. Unity is pursued at the price of knowing what we believe, for taking stands on theological issues can divide. Our increased attendance is offered as proof of the correctness of this view.

There are three major problems with such indifference to doctrine. First, it is unbiblical. Paul, for example, is not the least bit hesitant to proclaim the doctrine that God revealed to him. One of God's primary purposes in giving us the Bible is to reveal his nature and ways to us. To ignore the doctrinal aspects of Scripture in order to avoid disagreement is to trivialize the wonderful gift of God's revelation.

Second, making God knowable only through individual experience apart from objective truth is to fall prey to the postmodern ways of thought that we have just discussed. While we might not make the connection, the Christian distaste for taking doctrinal stands flows from our falling for secular opinion that Truth is unknowable and unimportant relative to experience.

The third reason is the most relevant to our purposes. We lose our children to secular ways of life and thinking because we fail to teach them that there is absolute truth. The biblical revelation of God offers us the information we need to build a comprehensive worldview that organizes our thinking and behaviour. This comprehensiveness is what our children need if they are to see the fullness of God's greatness and to be strengthened against the tantalizing offers of the devil. Our failure to value and teach the full counsel of God is a central reason that our children are weak in the faith. We would do well to heed Paul's advice in Romans 12:2: 'Do not conform any longer to the pattern of this world, but be transformed by the renewing of your mind.'

POSTMODERNISM AND THE LOSS OF HUMANNESS

A favourite target of Christian criticism is 'secular humanism'. This, as you know, is the view that humans are the ultimate value. It is a school of thought that formed a part of the Enlightenment thinking we described above, claiming that man, the apex of evolution, is able to solve all of his problems. Just as faith in the pursuit of knowledge has turned to despair, so has the newest view of humanity called postmodernism. Humans were dethroned from the centre of thought and there is now no centre

at all, each person creating his or her own. In thi
thinking, humans are not special, but merely a spe
all others. As Ingrid Newkirk, president of People fe
Treatment of Animals, said, 'A rat is a pig is a dog
follows that people lament the suffering of animal
the moral ills of society. Sacrificing rats for medica. ..ocurcii to
prolong the lives of humans becomes unethical and a form of
'species-ism'. On what basis dare we value human life more than
other forms?

This view of the equal status of all species is a basis for the
increased assault on the protected state of children. If we are
not special, why protect our little ones? If personal gain is our
greatest value, then why not tap the market inherent in children
and youth? Once upon a time children were somewhat safe
from commercialism. Now, cartoons are based on films that are
promoted through fast-food establishments. The line between
the entertainment and the products has blurred as media moguls
exploit parental guilt and coax children to get their parents to
buy them more 'stuff'. This invasion of our families becomes
even more blatant as children grow older. Commercial forces
appeal to the rebellious and even angry side of teens to promote
music and products that pull young people away from parents,
all the while expecting the parents to supply the money to make
it happen.

Children provide another focus for postmodern apathy for
humans. Gene Edward Veith, Jr., notes, 'The new anti-humanism
is inevitably anti-child, assuming as it does that new human life
is a problem, a drain on the earth and on the parents' resources.'[3]
Abortion is the proving ground for this view. Evangelical rhetoric
again misses the point. The issue is not really that unborn children
are alive, but that the choice of the individual is sovereign and
that human life is disposable if it interferes with free choice. After
all, abortion saves society from 'unwanted children' (a term that
in itself shows the devaluing of human life) and the financial and
emotional burden they impose.

So, when we see angry teenagers today, maybe we can understand them a bit better as they react against the implicit message
many of them receive: they are not really valued. In contrast,
Christians who understand this will be in a position to assert the
biblical view of humans, and children in particular, which places

great value on life because humans are made in the image of God and children are to be seen as gifts from him.

CHILDREN AS ADULTS

We have already seen how children are not protected as they used to be, especially in the media. The world is energetically recruiting its next generation of consumers.

I sometimes try to imagine life in days gone by. Only a few generations back a home was a private island. Though people interacted with their immediate community, parents easily controlled the intrusion of foreign ideas. Even so, foreign ideas were few as church, school and the community generally shared the same values, especially in Christian nations. Not so today. Even as I write, the air I breathe is filled with radio and television waves, beaming messages into my home that are completely unfit for children and go against everything I, as a father, am trying to teach my offspring. These evils are only a flip of a switch or click of a computer mouse away. The people who control such powerful influences have little respect for the vulnerability of children, seeing them as 'adults' who can make up their own minds.

A similar assault on children is seen in the area of sexuality. Situation comedies on television, often marketed as family fare, carry strong sexual messages to children. Occasionally this is done in a self-justified air of encouraging the public debate. Children are not only unprotected, but are portrayed as instigators of disrespect. Rude remarks from little ones are guaranteed laughs. Teenage sexuality is even more overtly depicted in programmes targeted at adolescents. The child who has liberal access to television is in many ways no longer a child at all.

Violence is promoted as well. While cartoons have admittedly always had violence in them, recently this has become much more graphic. The cheering of violence offers a false sense of empowerment to many youngsters who huddle in their inner-city homes, seeking safety from the all-too-real danger in the streets outside. Recent news of teenagers going on shooting rampages in the USA underscores the fact that children are adults when it comes to knowing violence.

Modern culture also encourages children to stand up for themselves, assuming they are equipped to handle adult issues and problems. Increasingly media depictions of children have them rebelling against parents who are portrayed as mentally dull and out of touch with the world. The immensely successful movie *Home Alone* and its sequels tapped into the fear of abandonment latent in the minds of many children, especially in a day when they may sense that their parents see them as inconveniences. The swash-buckling star of the show sends these children the message that children must, and can, fend for themselves against threatening adults. After all, you can't count on your parents to be there for you.

It is then clear that we are not bringing up children in a neutral environment, but one that sees our children as adults to be seduced into the ways of the world. We must be able to produce children who are not only able to stand against such forces, but to claim enemy territory for the cause of Christ. This cannot be accomplished with shallow thinking about their nature and nurture.

Fallout in the church

Our challenge is great enough, but the intrusion of these trends into the church itself makes it even greater. As those around us forsake truth, we retreat from the historic faith of the church to offer a weak faith of warm fuzzies. We hear of the loss of humanness as we count the numbers of persons who come to our churches and the dollars they leave behind. Good music and entertaining preaching abound, but genuine caring for persons, much less children, is rare. We may not be as inclined to treat our children as adults, but our indifference to this subtle worldly trend to do so betrays the shallowness of our thinking.

Lessons from the past

Our review of these contemporary trends shows that we have, indeed, underestimated the opposition, focusing our efforts for our children on the symptoms rather than on the deeper problems. We realize now that the historic Christian faith is not as 'at home' in the world as it may have been in days gone by. Truly biblical thinking goes contrary to the ways of the culture around us, and trying to make it fit isn't going to work. If we are to pass the faith on to our children, we must face the fact that true Christianity has been disenfranchised from our communities. Those genuinely burdened for our children must stop trying to fit the culture and realize that we must rediscover the unique Christian way of thinking and living.

In John Sommerville's intriguing book on children in English Puritan life, he points out that social groups lacking a secure place in the social structure are the most likely to sense the importance of reaching their children. The Puritans were such a group, and responded vigorously. Sommerville explains:

> Puritan books had to warn children against a society in which their brand of religion was unfashionable. By way of insuring commitment to the movement, puritan authors emphasized doctrinal purity and spiritual inner direction when they addressed young readers. In effect they offered children a base in religious authority from which to challenge a corrupt social authority.[4]

The Puritans saw themselves as a separate group, and possessed a well-defined theology to pass on. These are two advantages they have over many modern Christians. We must not simply react against aspects of culture we do not like, but reject it at its roots, replacing it with a more fully biblical worldview. We must, like the Puritans, have a thorough respect for our opposition, for the threats we face from our culture are greater than the ones they faced.

Serious times demand strong medicine: responding to the challenge

Why do we need another book on Christian ministry to children? The first part of the answer is, as we saw, that we have underestimated the adversity we face in raising children for Christ. The second part of the answer is that we have thus responded with shallow, 'how to' approaches that fail to consider the full counsel of Scripture. It is the purpose of this book to examine the entire teaching of the Bible that relates to children, to systematize it, and use this foundation to develop strategies that more adequately enable us to minister effectively to our children.

Thinking deeply about children and doctrine reminds me of spinach pie. I have never eaten such, and frankly the thought isn't particularly appetizing to me. Some things just don't seem to fit together well. Spinach has its place. A necessary evil, a 'good-for-you' food that many of us simply tolerate because we know we should. A few special souls develop a genuine taste for it, and I commend them for achieving something I have not. Pie, on the other hand, is a more pleasant topic. Sweetness, warmth, delight—all seem to go with the thought of this wonderful dessert. Spinach and pie appear to lack anything in common other than being edible, so the suggestion of a 'spinach pie' doesn't seem particularly palatable.

The notion of mixing the topics of children and theology also strikes us as incongruous and maybe even distasteful. In many Christian circles, the word 'theology' evokes a response much like our reaction to spinach. Images of ancient scholars come to mind, cloistered away in a monastery, writing Latin with a quill pen. Many of us never choose to 'consume' theology unless it is out of a sense of ought, and then only rarely. We easily view theology as too abstract and irrelevant in a day when the 'practical' aspects of the Christian religion are perceived as more tasteful.

In contrast, children, like pie, bring to mind warm and cheerful thoughts. We visualize children at play, discovering a butterfly or giggling during a game of tag. Theirs is a world quite distant from the intellectual musings of the theologian. Children are the dessert of life, a gift of God to sweeten the taste of our existence.

It is not surprising, then, to learn that little has been written about children from a theological perspective. While there is an abundance of literature on Christian parenting, virtually all of it fails to examine the foundations of our understanding of children that the Bible provides. The Bible certainly gives directions to parents, but it offers much more. It speaks of the importance of children, their spiritual nature, their sinfulness and need for salvation, their behavioural tendencies, and their place in the Christian church. Yet these topics have gone largely ignored given our present day eagerness to find what works to make children behave.

This book is written to address this need for well-founded thought about caring for our children. I believe that a firm understanding of all the Bible teaches about children, placed into a theological framework, will provide the only sufficient basis upon which to build methods of ministering to our children in our homes and churches. It is in such weighty reflection that we will find the full wealth of biblical counsel needed to protect our children in these ungodly days. The ills of the time demand serious medicine, and it is to be found in the 'spinach pie' I call a theology of children.

Preparing for the journey

We are about to embark on an enlightening journey through the biblical teachings about children, and in doing so will be preparing ourselves to reach out to those little ones under our care. But a warning is in order before we begin. Let me explain. We observed earlier that secular thought has despaired of finding truth, and rightly so given its failure to consider the spiritual. Its response was to declare that there is no absolute truth to be found. No-one, then, is right nor is anyone wrong in forming ideas about what is. We saw that Christians have followed further down this path than we would wish, surrendering scriptural doctrine for the sake of a user-friendly gospel.

If we are to give full credit to all that the Bible says about children, we will have to tread on some admittedly delicate terrain. It will take us into issues that have caused controversy through the history of the church, and I have no expectation that mine will be the final word. I am a fallen creature and am quite confident that my thinking will undergo correctives when I reach my Father's house. (That is not to mention that I will undoubtedly change some of my conclusions as I continue to study during my life here on earth!)

But we are not like secular scholars. As believers in absolute truth, we know that there are correct answers for all of the areas we will cover. Only our sin and fallen reason hide them from us. So, while I admit this book is not the final word, it is offered as a starting point for discussion. I believe that what you are about to read is a reasonably accurate description of what the Bible teaches, or I would not offer it to the public. I will undoubtedly upset some people with some of my conclusions. I won't be surprised if most people disagree with me at some points. This is a step toward the perfect truth of the counsel of God and, like any human interpretation, will fall short.

I ask you, the reader, to enter with an open mind. In discussing such topics as the fate of children dying in infancy, I have found many people to have strong sentiments but yet give little thought to why they hold them. You might reconsider your opinions. Some of you come from different denominational traditions and will not agree with my positions. I ask you to respond by giving thought to how you would develop a theology of children from your tradition. Believing that there is only one truth, I don't believe we can both be right, but I am confident there is great value in considering the nature and nurture of children from different perspectives as we share the goal of discerning the perfect truth of God.

I strongly encourage the reader prayerfully to consider the passages to be discussed and to read this book thoughtfully. I especially ask that you seek God's guidance in applying what you read to your work with children in whatever capacity you serve. I believe you will emerge from your time with this book with a new vision for children and new tools for ministry to them.

Who needs a theology of children?

This leads to the final point of our introductory chapter, and that is to establish who might profit from this study. I believe there is benefit here for those who teach future pastors and teachers in higher education classes, and maybe even a theologian or two will be stimulated to reflect on the importance of children in the general study of theology.

Ministers are responsible for the spiritual care of their entire flocks, and that doubtlessly includes the little lambs. Pastors need to understand fully the matters affecting the care of their youngest and weakest members. (Whether children should be considered as 'members' of the church is a matter we will address later.) It is pastors who are often called at the birth of a child, who preside over the baptism or dedication of infants, who are consulted when children make a profession of faith, who are called upon for counsel by troubled parents, and who introduce children into the membership of the church at the appropriate time. Pastors provide leadership to the church's governing body that is charged with providing a suitable context for education in the faith while at church, and encourage parents to do the same with their children at home. All those in ministry will do well to consider the discussion that follows. There is much to be said that can lead to a more faithful church ministry to children.

Yet, the 'front line' responsibility for the nurture of children rests with their parents, and the vital nature of the task of parenting challenges us to meet it with a thorough understanding of the place of children in the eyes of God. Similarly, other believers who minister to children can profit and enhance their work by this study. This includes church leaders and educators of all types, such as Sunday school teachers, school teachers, and home school teachers. The same applies to those who perform other 'professional' functions for children, such as physicians, counsellors, tutors and care-givers. Of course, all believers have a stake in the new generation, for it is the future of the church. In most churches all the members vow to participate in the lives of its children at dedications or baptisms, and Christian nurture is a task that falls to the body as a whole.

Our Covenant with Kids is addressed to all the faithful who are burdened for our children and their nurture in our churches and our homes. We see the vicious threats posed by the world around us and confess our piecemeal approaches to meeting the challenge of our children. We are eager to hear what the Word of God says about our little ones and to understand it as best we can. Only then will we be ready to develop strategies for ministry that adequately address their needs and lead them toward the faith. We commit ourselves to our children, for of such is the kingdom of God.

2

BLESSINGS, NOT BURDENS

'Sons are a heritage from the LORD, *children a reward from him.'*
(Psalm 127:3)

*'He gives children, not as a penalty nor as a burden, but as
a favour'* (C. H. Spurgeon).

*'We know the worth of dead, or rather lifeless treasures, but who
knows the worth of living treasures?'* (Joseph Caryl).

Imagine you are an ancient Spartan, making the routine walk to
the town rubbish heap. As you approach this aromatic locale you
are distracted by a faint cry. You shift your direction and quicken
your pace. As you draw near the small form, your expectations
are realized: another child has been deserted by its parents, left to
die or possibly be rescued. The practice of exposure is thriving.

Our modern sensibilities are appalled at the thought of
exposing a child, though this was actually the more humane of
the options available in ancient times for those who didn't care
to keep their children. The town dump was a frequent choice for
leaving unwanted infants as it was relatively private, and there
was a chance some one would be moved enough to take the child
home. In a day where fathers had legal rights to life or death

for their children, exposure was a relatively kind alternative to infanticide, though those taking in exposed children frequently raised them for prostitution. Children were often seen as inconveniences or burdens, problems to be disposed of rather than tolerated.

One needs look no further than the pages of Scripture for evidence that people can be heartless toward children. Pharaoh, king of Egypt, thought the murder of all male babies of the Hebrews to be a fair price to ease his anxiety about the growth of this group of slaves (Exod. 1:15–22). God later served justice on Egypt as he slew their firstborn in the last of the ten plagues. Herod tried a similar strategy (Matt. 2:13–23) to protect himself from the threat of the newborn King. Herod met his end none the less, and the infant King changed history.

People have been cruel to children throughout history. Children have frequently been sacrificed to pagan gods, used as sexual toys, or served as objects on which to vent frustrations. Abortion is not new either, for children have a long history of being 'unwanted'. This practice sounds more familiar to us today, for millions have chosen to abort babies in our lifetimes, mostly because they are considered to be inconvenient (a motive less understandable than that of Pharaoh and Herod!). Child abuse, both physical and sexual, is still rampant, though at least these practices remain illegal. The sacrifice or abuse of children has long been a core practice of those who worship Satan as they seek to act completely contrary to the Christian respect for children. History presents a strong argument that children are not universally valued and appreciated; a trend that holds very true today.

The perception of children in history has been varied. In contrast to the practices of exposure and infanticide, there have been times when the dominant philosophy of cultures has been pro-children. Children have been idealized over the past two centuries in particular, being put on pedestals of innocence to offer hope in contrast to an increasingly corrupt adult society. Children's advocates today work for children's rights, sometimes to the point of infringing on parents' rights or common sense. Government regulations invade the home to the extent that parents worry about disciplining their children or teaching them their beliefs for fear of having them taken away. Paradoxically, these views hold sway while unborn children are deemed inhuman and naïve children are prey for slick marketing executives.

This paradoxical resentment and idealization of children betrays the historical ambivalence humans feel toward children. There is generally a natural attraction to our offspring. Many adults find satisfaction in parenting. Others see joy in the carefree playfulness of children, even to the point of living their own lives irresponsibly to be like them. But children present a financial, emotional and time-consuming responsibility that does not fit well with the radical individualism of our day. Many couples take advantage of new birth-control technologies to avoid parenthood at all costs. Choice in this matter is valued over life. Yet, those who have children often indulge them materially in an attempt to assuage the guilt they feel for resenting the imposition the children make into already hectic lives.

The media perpetuate this paradox. As we have noted, children are depicted as clever and resourceful while parents are buffoons. Children are no longer childlike and innocent, but are portrayed as sexual objects, lovers of violence and disillusioned with any notion of authority.

It is into this world where our neighbours do not know what to think of children and lack any sense of mission or direction in their parenting that we as Christians are to present the biblical view of children. The Bible and church history portray a decidedly different perception and understanding of children than that of the world around us.

Special gifts from the King

One cannot get past the first verse of the Bible without seeing that God is the Author of creation, and brings into being what he chooses. Accidents are not possible with God. In Deuteronomy 32:39 God specifically informs us that

> See now that I myself am He! There is no god besides me.
> I put to death and I bring to life...

If God is in absolute control (and if he is not, he is something other than God), and if he is the one who gives life, then the conception of a new human life must be seen as a divine act of grace and generosity.

This idea is made explicit in Psalm 127:3 as quoted at the beginning of this chapter. Here is the foundational truth about the value and significance of children: they are divine gifts. We shall examine later the nature of these gifts and will see more completely why they are to be cherished. For now, we will focus on the plain truth that the people of God have always sought, cared for, nurtured, protected, loved, and trained children in light of their being perceived as signs of divine favour. As Calvin comments, 'Children are not the fruit of chance, but… God, as it seems good to him, distributes to every man his share of them.'[1]

Here is an essential word to be spoken into a world that exhibits intensely mixed feelings toward children. God Almighty wills each individual birth of a child, with each being seen as his gift of grace to the parents. Spurgeon accurately observed, 'Where society is rightly ordered children are regarded, not as an encumbrance, but as an inheritance; and they are received, not with regret, but as a reward.'[2] This attitude stands in contrast to the frustrated reaction of many today when they learn they are to become parents.

Calvin outlines the significance of this truth for parenting:

> How inexcusable will be the impiety of men, if when he [God] adorns them with the honourable title of fathers, they account this favour as nothing…. Unless men regard their children as the gift of God, they are careless and reluctant in providing for their support, just as on the other hand this knowledge contributes in a very eminent degree to encourage them in bringing up their offspring.[3]

Thus, a thorough understanding of children being gifts from God is the basis for all our interaction with our children and those of others. The Bible makes clear that the proper emotional response to having children is happiness (Ps. 127:5) as we realize the wonder of God graciously giving us such gifts. Those who do not know God as Sovereign are sadly deprived of this blessed truth, leaving them vulnerable to lower views of childbearing. So, let's ponder the biblical theme of children as gifts so we might strengthen our understanding of the Christian attitude toward children.

GIFTS OF TWO TYPES

Male children have historically been valued more than females. Boys would provide heirs and continuity of the family line while guaranteeing a source of labour for the family business. Daughters were sometimes helpful, but generally the birth of a daughter was a disappointment to parents. The biblical data tell a different story, for the people of God were elated to receive any child as a gift of God. While one cannot miss the significance of the birth of sons, we also see joy associated with having daughters.

The Hebrew term *ben* is used over 5,000 times in the Old Testament and typically was a generic reference to children of both sexes, though more particularly it means 'son' or 'group member'. The context makes the particular meaning of *ben* clear in individual passages, yielding ample evidence that the birth of sons made for happy parents. Sons were important for the simple reason that they continued the father's line, as seen in Deuteronomy 25:5-10 where details are given for preserving a man's lineage. They often received special blessings from their fathers (Gen. 27:28-9; 48:14-22), the firstborn in particular. After Israel's firstborn were spared in the Passover, the setting apart of the firstborn son became a ritual to remind the parents of the Lord's bringing Israel out of Egypt, but also to serve as an instructional rite to the son. Circumcision, dating back to Abraham (Gen. 17:1-14), was a ritual related only to male offspring, again showing their religious significance. Special emphasis was given to instructing sons in the Law (Deut. 11:19), and this carried a particular blessing to parents (Deut. 11:21).

Yet, daughters are also valued in the Bible. We appeal first to God's sovereign decision to create woman in the first place (Gen. 2:18), giving women the inherent significance of fulfilling man's need for companionship. Daughters are, consequently, divinely ordained to fulfil this ongoing purpose in creation. If God is sovereign over all births, then he is no less active in ordaining the birth of daughters. Girls too can perform labour valuable to the family, these services being nicely summarized in Proverbs 31:10-31. The physical labour of daughters is readily seen in passages such as Genesis 24:15-20, where Rebekah carries water for her family and for Abraham's servant, and Genesis 29:9 which depicts Rachel's vocation as a shepherdess. The fourth commandment explicitly includes daughters in the list of those who are to receive the benefit of Sabbath rest (Exod. 20:10), implying that they were active in labour. So, it is unmistakable that children of both sexes are valuable tokens of God's goodness.

GIFTS WE DON'T WANT TO LOSE

Given the great value placed on children in Scripture, the Bible contains a noteworthy theme of concern for the health and life of little ones. Our relative confidence in the survival of our children is a fairly modern one, for high infant mortality rates have been more the rule than the exception throughout history. One might understand if many parents would distance themselves from their children to protect against grief should the child not make it. Not so in the Bible.

We can infer from the Genesis 4 account of the first 'dysfunctional family' that Adam and Eve mourned the loss of their second-born son Abel, with their grief undoubtedly exacerbated by awareness that their other son had perpetrated the murder. Though Joseph was not in truth dead, this was the deception perpetrated by his brothers on their father, Jacob. Genesis 37:34–5 depicts the depth of his grief as Jacob 'mourned for his son many days', refusing to be comforted by the rest of his family. Profound love indeed yields profound grief. In 2 Samuel 12:15–23 we read of the illness of David's illegitimate child by Bathsheba, and David's wrenching grief and petition for this child's life. Evil King Jeroboam was burdened by the illness of his son Abijah (1 Kings 14:1–3) but the death of the child was inevitable according to God's prophet, Ahijah (1 Kings 14:6–13).

The widow whose son dies in 1 Kings 17:7–24 grieves mightily, but is graciously given back her son through the prophet Elijah. Job was truly a family man, taking great care to consecrate his children just in case they had 'sinned and cursed God in their hearts' (Job 1:5). It must have been devastating when these children were taken from him in a great wind. Remarkably, Job's response is not only to grieve, but also to worship (Job 1:20–22). Luke's Gospel provides accounts of Jesus raising a widow's son from the dead (7:12–17) followed by the more familiar account of his restoring the life of Jairus' daughter (8:41–2, 49–56). Our

Saviour surely showed great compassion for the pain of grieving parents.

The emotional trauma of the death of a child is as great as any that we endure. This gives us cause to reflect on the wondrous grace of our God who gave his Son voluntarily to die for our sins. Such amazing love should move us to praise and to assurance as we say with Paul, 'He who did not spare his own Son, but gave him up for us all—how will he not also, along with him, graciously give us all things?' (Rom. 8:32).

Potent anxious feelings befall parents of seriously ill children. John 4:46–54 tells of the royal official whose son was sick and at the point of death. Jesus speaks, and the boy is healed. Matthew (15:22–8) and Mark (7:24–30) describe the faith of the Syro-Phoenician woman whose daughter was 'cruelly demon-possessed'. This account offers several significant insights for our study. First, note that Scripture here demonstrates that a child can be possessed by a demon, a fact which reveals the importance of the spirituality of children and gives us cause to be more aggressive in prayers for the protection of our children. Secondly, observe the heart of a mother and Jesus' compassion in a culture where fathers were the ones with power. Jesus responds to the great faith of this woman and immediately heals her daughter.

The number of instances of Jesus showing mercy to parents and children in his earthly ministry confirms in our mind that children are not only prized by parents, but by our Lord.

PROMISED GIFTS

Since God determines the birth of children inasmuch as they are gifts from him, it follows that he would be in a position to promise children when he sees fit. The Bible demonstrates that this is indeed the case.

The first promised birth is the most significant. In Genesis 3:15, God is cursing the serpent and informs him that there will be enmity between his seed and that of the woman. This is almost universally understood as a reference to the birth of God's Son, Jesus Christ. Numerous Old Testament prophecies testify to the coming birth of the Messiah (e.g. Isaiah 7:14), and the New Testament accounts are quick to point this out. An angel announced the promised birth to the mother-to-be in Luke 1:28–38, and subsequently to her fiancé in Matthew 1:20–21.

A promised child is an essential element of God's covenant with Abram. A general promise of offspring is made in Genesis 12:1–9, followed by a more explicit word in 17:16. Isaac, the promised child, is eventually born 'at the very time God had promised' (Gen. 21:2).

Angels were active in announcing such special births. This was noted with regard to Jesus, and is also seen in Judges 13 as the angel of the Lord announced to the barren wife of Manoah that she would have a son. An angelic messenger (John 1) also foretold the birth of Jesus' cousin, John. God also can use a prophet to promise a child, as seen in the account of Elisha and the Shunammite woman (2 Kings 4:8–37).

These stories provide ample evidence that God is sovereign over the birth of children. Only one in control of childbearing is able to promise children. The God of truth is not in the business of promising what he cannot deliver, and his plans cannot be thwarted. These children were gratefully received as gifts, with declarations of joy and praise as seen, for example, in the song of Mary (Luke 1:46–55).

SOLITARY GIFTS: SINGLE CHILDREN

Given that parenthood is a divine gift, an only child is a special treasure, embodying all of the parents' hopes, dreams and emotions in one life. Scripture offers a touching assortment of stories about an only child. The story of Jephthah (Judg. 11:29–40) is a tragic place to begin. He rather impulsively promises to sacrifice the first thing to come out of the doors of his house, and that turns out to be his daughter: 'She was an only child. Except for her he had neither son nor daughter' (Judg. 11:34). Despite the horrible ending to this story, Jephthah is granted a place in the 'honour roll' of faith in Hebrews 11:32.

Luke's account of Jesus' ministry depicts the special concerns of parents of an only child, and Jesus as being quite compassionate toward these families. This can be observed in three accounts clustered together in Luke chapters 7–9. We noted two of these earlier, with Jesus raising two only children from the dead.

Luke 9:37–43 relates how Jesus cast out a demon from a man's only son after Jesus' disciples failed to do so.

It thus appears that the Word of God demonstrates a touching sensitivity to the plight of parents of an only child, showing particularly our Lord's graciousness toward the parents of a suffering only child. We in the church today will do well to pay special attention to the 'only begottens' in our midst.

The sorrow of childlessness

Almighty God, having completed his creation of the universe and his most favoured creatures, the man and woman, issues his first command to them: 'Be fruitful and increase in number' (Gen. 1:28). The divine mandate to bear children is issued before the Fall and before the giving of the Law, establishing it as a priority for the creatures made in God's likeness. Only Paul's brief allusion to the spiritual benefits of being single (1 Cor. 7:8) tempers the command to bear children. Bearing children is in most cases a form of obedience for the believer. This shows that God graciously gives children, at least in part, in response to those who seek to obey his command to be fruitful. The first human birth evokes from Eve praise to God as she understood this was 'with the help of the LORD' (Gen. 4:1). Jacob later commented to Esau that his children were gracious gifts of God (Gen. 33:5), confirming the divine role in childbearing. The command to 'be fruitful and increase in number' is reiterated after the flood (Gen. 9:7) to demonstrate its ongoing significance. Bearing children is thus a creation mandate and a primary purpose for marital sex. In a day where the pleasures of marital sex are frequently praised by Christian authors, we do well to remember that there is to be a pleasure beyond the pleasure: parenthood.

If children are God's gifts and rewards, then it follows that the lack of them can be punishment in some cases. Leviticus 20:20–21 explicitly states that childlessness is the penalty for sexual sin with wives of relatives. Michal, Saul's daughter, was childless following her jealous rebuke of David in 2 Samuel 6:20–23. Childlessness is prophesied as a punishment in Jeremiah 22:30, and 'wombs that miscarry and breasts that are dry' are prayed against Ephraim in Hosea 9:14, as is a curse of 'no birth, no pregnancy, no conception' in verse 11. This may sound somewhat strange in a day when many young couples would see this as a blessing and not a curse, as having children is not valued as highly as their other plans.

If parenthood was valued so highly, and barrenness often seen as a punishment, then to be without children was a cause for sorrow. Rachel's desperate plea to Jacob, 'Give me children, or I'll die!' (Gen. 30:1) is the most graphic example of the misery of childlessness seen in the Scriptures, but definitely it is not the only one. (Her lament was answered in verses 22–4, but she was still not satisfied, saying, 'May the LORD add to me another son.') The entire fiasco with Abram, Sarai and Hagar shows the lengths to which God's people would go to be parents, in this case failing to wait upon God's timing. Isaac prays for his barren wife, a prayer answered with Jacob and Esau (Gen. 25:21–6). The story of the Shunammite woman in 2 Kings 4, which we noted earlier, is also helpful to show that a woman can be barren without its being a specific punishment. Her son is given as a gift of gratitude for her care for Elijah and Gehazi. The intensity of the emotion around her barrenness is easily observed in verse 16 where she scorns the promise of Elijah, fearing the disappointment such a promise might bring. She was soon to learn the faithfulness of God. In the New Testament, Elizabeth saw her pregnancy with John as taking away the disgrace of her childlessness (Luke 1:25).

The biblical importance of bearing children is also seen in the rivalry fuelled by differing 'success rates'. Rachel was jealous of her sister Leah (Gen. 30:1), Sarai became resentful when Hagar bore Abram a son (Gen. 16:4–6), and Peninnah provoked Elkanah's other wife, Hannah, because 'the LORD had closed her womb' (1 Sam. 1:6). 1 Kings 3:16–28 shows the rivalry of two harlots who had begotten children, one of which had died. Solomon in his wisdom appealed to the natural affection of a mother to decide the matter, rightly assuming the true mother would give up her child rather than see him killed. Their desire for the child was great despite the potentially negative impact it would have on their 'careers'.

Let me be clear. While there are examples of barrenness being punishment from God, this is certainly not the case in many, if not most, instances. Childlessness today is a source of profound grief for many couples who would gladly fulfil the creation mandate if they could. Here is an important opportunity for the church to provide a much-needed ministry of support and encouragement as it reflects a biblical concern for childless couples.

The special joy of adoption

We cannot search the mind of God, and thus cannot apprehend his wisdom in depriving some couples of offspring while granting children to parents who do not want them. While many Christian couples work diligently to avoid having children, apparently oblivious to the divine mandate, other couples grieve their inability to bear children and often undergo considerable expense in an effort to become fertile. God has graciously provided the practice of adoption to provide consolation to childless couples and homes to children who are not wanted by their biological parents. This is not a new practice and has a strong biblical (and extrabiblical) history behind it. Let us review adoption as illustrated in Scripture.

Adoption often served the purpose of providing a male heir to a household, with servants or sons-in-law being adopted to this end. On occasion a couple might choose to die without an heir, and this was evidently the situation with Zacharias and Elizabeth (Luke 1:7), but this was the exception. While Abram was childless, he made the assumption that Eliezer of Damascus, apparently a slave, would be his heir (Gen. 15:2–3). According to ancient documents such as the Nuzi texts, this was common practice in that day, constituting a form of adoption.

Abram and Sarai also tried a second option available to childless couples, the use of a 'surrogate mother' in the person of a female slave. Hagar (Gen. 16) succeeded where Sarai had failed, but this child was not the child of promise and, as a result, Abram and Sarai (and future generations!) regretted their impatience. Genesis 30:3–8 describes this strategy as being the solution to the woes of childless Rachel. Jacob accurately reminded her that it was God who had withheld children from her (Gen. 30:2), but he cooperated with her plan to use her maid Bilhah, with two sons resulting. Her sister Leah followed suit when she realized she was barren, and utilized her maid Zilpah to bear two more sons for Jacob.

The patriarch who lacked a male heir might give a daughter to a servant to be his wife and thus bear heirs. This practice is seen briefly in 1 Chronicles 2:34–5 where Sheshan gave his daughter to his Egyptian servant Jarha and the couple bore an heir. This was an adoption in a sense, making one who was not a biological family member an heir.

Modern adoptions are more likely to be desired to produce the fulfilment of parenting rather than to provide an heir, though most young couples would do well to give more thought to the question of who will care for them in their old age and carry on the family name. The Bible offers two examples that are more typical of adoptions today. The story of Moses being spared from the massacre of infants and taken in by Pharaoh's daughter is a familiar one (Exod. 2:1–10), but the brief phrase in verse 10 'and he became her son' is often overlooked. Pharaoh's daughter, realizing full well that this was a Hebrew child (Exod. 2:6) whom her father had condemned, took him as her own and adopted him.

Esther was an orphan whose parents had died (Est. 2:7). Mordecai, Esther's first cousin, 'had taken her as his own daughter' upon the death of her parents. This adoption seems to have been a ministry to family, and is also noteworthy in that there is no mention of Mordecai being married, so we apparently see biblical precedent for a single adoptive parent.

While these examples of adoption in the Bible are very instructive, undoubtedly the primary illustration of the importance and value of adoption is found in the work of God himself in adopting us as his children.

We are not by nature children of God, though this stands in direct conflict with much modern religious folklore. Sinful man is not in a filial relationship with his Creator, for sin itself establishes a barrier. While God by nature is Creator, he is only Father by virtue of the redeeming work of Christ. It is by the work of Christ on the cross in bearing our sins that we are declared righteous and God's wrath averted, but it is the doctrine of adoption that establishes us as children of God. It is marvellous that God has made provision for our sins, but it is even more astounding that he has adopted us to be his children. We rejoice with John: 'How great is the love the Father has lavished on us, that we should be called the children of God! And that is what we are' (1 John 3:1). This separates us from those around us, however, as he adds: 'The reason the world does not know us is that it did not know him.'

If our spiritual standing and security rests on God's adopting us, it immediately follows that adoption of children is a way to follow our heavenly Father's lead. It is altogether fitting that Christians lead in efforts to adopt 'unwanted' children, doing for others (in a sense) as God has done for us. This is motivation above the acquiring of an heir, meeting a 'felt need' to parent, or reaching out to unloved and unwanted children. It is a visible way that we demonstrate to the world around us a shadow of what our heavenly Father has done for us.

Our response to God's generosity

If the teaching of Scripture stresses the worth of the lives of children, it follows that Christians should live in such a way as to value the lives of little ones.

DEFENDING THE LIVES OF CHILDREN

Early Christian writings establish the outworking of the biblical view of children in contrast to the surrounding culture. Justin, one of the earliest fathers, spoke of exposure as a 'sin against God'.[4] Tertullian, writing around 200, attacks abortion as a form of infanticide, saying,

> To hinder a birth is merely a speedier man-killing; nor does it matter whether you take away a life that is born, or destroy one that is coming to the birth. That is a man which is going to be one; you have the fruit already in its seed.[5]

Our tradition of defending the lives of children thus dates to our beginnings. As modern times have produced a resurgence in the practice of abortion, it is again our duty to speak against it and to offer options to pregnant women. These may take the form of making it feasible for them to keep their babies or providing for adoption. The issue of whether unborn infants are 'lives' or 'choices' gains greater focus when we see them as living gifts from God.

ADOPTING UNWANTED CHILDREN

We've seen the powerful biblical theme of adoption, and this certainly should lead to practice as we prayerfully consider whether God would have us adopt or help others who are trying to do so. International adoptions have become more plentiful and open new doors to ministering to children without families. Children in foster care are often available for adoption, though they often prove more challenging. Finally, serving as foster parents can be a meaningful ministry to displaced children, offering them a place in a Christian home. Churches would do well to consider how God might have them support families in their churches who adopt by specific prayer, financial support and encouragement.

ENCOURAGING THE CHILDLESS

Given the agony suffered by many childless couples, Christian individuals, couples and churches can ease the pain through compassionate ministry. This sometimes rests on the willingness of the hurting couple to share their pain, but this should be easier if they know they are in a caring Christian community.

CARING FOR THE SICK AND DYING

One of my most influential learning experiences was working in a hospital for children with cancer. Often the fear and sorrow of a seriously ill child pull families apart rather than together. Sick and dying children, with their families, are most appropriate subjects for Christian ministry, and church leaders would do well to consider better how to reach these hurting children and families, especially those within the church.

TREASURING OUR GIFTS IN HOME AND CHURCH

We have learned that children are gifts, tokens of God's grace. As parents, we are thus challenged to be more grateful to the Giver of these gifts, and to be better stewards of them. What worthier goal of parenting than to raise children to live to the glory of the One who breathed life into them? On a corporate level, we are challenged to care more faithfully for the little ones in our churches. As children of God, we are brothers and sisters to each other and all our children are family. May we think more carefully about what this means to our lives as individual families and churches. The remainder of this book will get us started in this process.

INNOCENTS OR DEVILS?
THE SPIRITUAL NATURE OF CHILDREN

'Surely I was sinful at birth, sinful from the time my mother conceived me.' (Psalm 51:5)

'God made man a little lower than the angels, and he's been getting lower and lower ever since' (Will Rogers).

The scene is all too typical. A heartbroken and discouraged pair of Christian parents crumble into my office chairs and share their disillusionment about their children. The father begins, 'I've really had it. I have spanked our kids whenever they did wrong or upset us, and they still are rebellious.'

'Doctor,' the mother interjects, 'my husband and I have argued about the kids for years. He insists they be spanked for any little thing they've done wrong: "Spare the rod and spoil the child." I disagree. I think we are to be loving and understanding, forgiving their mistakes.'

'Either way, they're ungrateful and flat out sinful. The wife and I agree on one thing: we've failed as parents, and I guess as Christians as well.'

The mother laments, 'I always believed if we loved our children, protected their self-esteem, and provided them with a good life that they would grow to be obedient and respectful. At least that's what I've read in some parenting books.'

The doleful faces of this exhausted couple prick my heart. Here are two well-intended believers who take raising children seriously and have pursued the ideas they thought right only to give themselves failing marks as their children begin to mature. Oh, sure, it is easy to fault them for being divided, and that certainly hasn't helped matters. But how can two sincere Christians have such differing views of how to raise children, neither of which seems successful?

The answer is surprisingly simple: by adopting parenting techniques without understanding exactly why they are supposed to work. We in the West are a pragmatic bunch. Tell us how to do it and don't slow us down with explanations. Give us 'how' and don't bother with 'why'. As a result, we end up with lots of strategies but are not really sure why they should work. For Christian parents this results in basing our approach to raising children on unexamined assumptions of what we are working with and trying to accomplish. Most often these assumptions are tied to the Bible in some way, but fail to incorporate the 'big picture' of all that Scripture has to say about children and raising them.

The couple above demonstrates two common approaches. The father epitomizes the authoritarian model that says that if you are forceful enough your kids will respect you. The biblical 'basis' for this was mentioned in our vignette: a narrow view of parenting as 'Spare the rod and spoil the child'. He proudly defends the Bible's endorsement of the 'rod' but fails to see there is more to be learned. For example, this strategy doesn't give us much idea as to why children need the 'rod' or how it is to be used. (We'll examine this in depth in chapter 7.)

The mother is more contemporary, believing that kindness begets kindness. Children, being basically sweet-natured, will blossom without really needing punishment. This is a form of the self-esteem view which claims that behaviour problems only occur when a child doesn't feel good about herself. Children who are confident in themselves will naturally behave well. Parents strive to be sure their children are happy and protect them from anything that might make them think less of themselves. Christians often rationalize this by pointing out that if we are to love our neighbour as ourselves, we've got to be sure we love ourselves well enough first.

These approaches at least are based on some sort of logic. Others are more personal and spontaneous, generally being reactions to the way one was raised himself: 'My parents did it that way and I turned out all right,' or 'I promised myself I'd never treat my kids the way I was treated' are examples of this view. Others parent by their feelings, punishing children when angered by their behaviour or 'attitudes'. Still others fly by the seat of their pants and have no strategy but respond to provocation in one way this time and another way the next.

All of these approaches fall short because they don't build on a thoroughly biblical understanding of what children are like. This leads us to a major theme of this book: Parenting techniques must flow from a biblical understanding of the nature of children. If I am to wire a house for electricity, I had better not just dive into the task. Rather, I need to learn how electricity works lest I hurt myself and destroy the very house I'm working on. Wiring outlets and running cable is not hard, but making sure these are compatible with the nature of the electrical current that will run through them requires a thorough understanding of electricity. In the same way, Christian parents need to have a biblical view of children before choosing their approaches to parenting so their plans compliment the spiritual nature of their children.

The roots of popular thought

Weeds are pesky because their roots are strong and hidden. So it is with the ideas many Christians have about the nature of children: they are difficult to eliminate because their roots in secular psychology are strong and well hidden even from those who hold them. Let's look at two major views and examine their roots so we can remove them from the garden of our ideas about the nature of children.

Easily the most popular is the view that children are naturally good (or sinless) until they are exposed to the problems of the world and do wrong as a response to the bad things of society. This view became almost automatic to Westerners by the huge success of *Baby and Child Care* by Dr Benjamin Spock (not the one with pointy ears on Star Trek) and Thomas Gordon's *Parent Effectiveness Training*. Both of these books are deeply embedded in humanism that stresses that people are by nature good. Many Christians have absorbed this view into their thinking without realizing it, assuming that children are good from birth but may mess up later on.

The behavioural psychologists, led by authorities like B. F. Skinner, see children as 'blank slates' when they arrive in the world, tending toward neither good nor bad. Parents and others in the environment determine the child's personality by their reactions to the child's behaviour. Little ones learn to be good or bad, depending upon what they are taught. Many if not most Christians hold this view today in a form which teaches that children are born morally innocent and, until they sin, deserve to go to heaven if they die because they have no failures on their records. Children eventually become accountable for their behaviour once they understand the difference between right and wrong. Yet, they inevitably sin in fulfilment of the biblical statement that 'all have sinned' (Rom. 3:23). This view sees children as beginning neutral but as eventually sinning in some way.

Neither of these views clearly reflects the teaching of Scripture, so parenting approaches based on them will fail to meet the true spiritual needs of children and lead to disappointments such as those of the couple we met earlier. As Christians we must take care to examine our ideas before putting them into action lest we see 'weeds' sprout from what we've planted. We need to delay the 'how to' strategies until we have a better understanding of who we are dealing with. Let us expose and uproot the 'weeds' in our thinking and look to the pure Word of God to learn about the spiritual nature of children.

Created in his image

What makes us so special anyway? Why do Christians value human life over other forms? The answer is found in Genesis 1:26. Whereas God declared that the rest of his creation was good, man stands above the rest by being expressly created in the image of God. This is not the same as saying that all people are the children of God, for that is a title reserved for God's special people. Rather, the image of God defines the uniqueness that sets us apart from all other creatures. It then follows that when we minister to a child, we need to appreciate the meaning of this little one being made in the image of God.

Our task of understanding the spiritual nature of children requires us to answer two vital questions about the image of God. First, what exactly does it mean that we are made in God's image? Second, we know that Adam and Eve sinned after they were created in the likeness of God, so how is the image evident in the lives of people who live after the fall of Adam?

Of what does the image consist?

Frankly, there is no definitive answer to our first question. Many writers have spoken of the 'riddle' of the content of the image because the biblical evidence is so scanty.[1] This means that a variety of opinions have been offered as to what the image is, and I encourage the ambitious reader to study these further on his or her own. I will present what I believe to be the best explanation.

Since Genesis doesn't come right out and tell us what the image is, how are we to know? John Calvin declares that 'the end of regeneration is that Christ should reform us to God's image'.[2] What-ever the image was, it was fouled up when Adam sinned. But once we are born again, it is to be restored through sanctification and glorification. If we know what has to be restored to the image after we are saved, we know of what it consisted before Adam sinned.

The New Testament gives us two verses that suggest the nature of the image of God in this manner. Colossians 3:10 states we 'have put on the new self, which is being renewed in knowledge in the image of its Creator'. Paul here teaches that the image of the Creator includes knowledge, suggesting our capacity for knowing to be one way in which we are made in God's image. This is not a new interpretation as it can be traced at least as far back as the fifth century when Augustine claimed 'reason and intelligence' to be part of the divine image in man.[3] Given that God is all-knowing, being in his image would include some share of this knowledge. This makes much logical sense as no-one debates that man is far superior to the animals in intelligence.

Language serves as a good example of human intellectual capacity. Our ability to communicate with each other opens the door to the thinking skills that make us human, such as reason, contemplation, and abstraction. God even reveals himself to us in language in the Bible, again showing the importance of our intelligence. Only man among the creatures is capable of knowing God, and only man is aware of himself. These, too, set us apart from the rest of creation.

What does this have to do with kids? A major part of the joy in watching children grow is seeing them grow in intelligence and language skills. Little children pick up language at an astounding speed, and researchers have learned that the brain appears to be created ready to be 'programmed' in any particular language to which the child is exposed. How do we teach our little ones about God or about what is right and wrong? We appeal to their ability to understand words and to reason out what is the right thing to do in particular situations. Indeed, adults invest more energy in trying to educate children than on almost any other thing. So it seems reasonable that being made in God's image includes being given the gift of intelligence by him.

The second aspect of God's image in man which we can deduce from Scripture also comes from the writings of Paul, this time from Ephesians 4:24. Paul says the new self is 'created to be like God in true righteousness and holiness'. 'Righteousness' and 'holiness' represent moral perfection, the former meaning one only does what is right and the latter reflecting purity of character and behaviour. Adam was righteous before he sinned, and as such he enjoyed sweet, unhindered fellowship with God. The first man always did that which was right, given his perfect moral nature. This also dramatically set Adam apart from the beasts that were governed merely by instinct.

Since God is holy and righteous, to be made in his image would reasonably include a moral component as is suggested in our text. Romans 8:29 tells us that believers are predestined to be conformed to the image of Christ, referring to Christ's sinlessness. Being pure like God is also the Christian's goal according to 1 John 3:1-3. Our restoration to the image of God then appears to mean a return to a state of moral perfection, one that Adam had at the dawn of human history. Adam sacrificed this perfection when he sinned, polluting his descendants as well. We continue to have a moral sense and inclination, but one which is now tarnished by sinful motives and distorted reasoning about what is right.

Children offer evidence of morality early on, as researchers have found basic forms of empathy (a moral emotion) in the tearful responses of infants to the sounds of other children in distress. Scientists such as Lawrence Kohlberg have devoted much energy to tracking the process of how children develop in their ability to reason morally. Whereas Kohlberg and other scholars admit human morality and study its growth, they offer no insight into what is moral or not. They strangely neglect the moral correctness of the choices people make, focusing purely on the processes used to make them. Nonetheless, there seems to be general agreement even in the secular realm that man has a moral inclination which we as Christians see as part of the image of God.

Let's take a moment to summarize what we have covered in this section. Children are born in the image of God. When Adam was first created, he shared in a great deal of knowledge and in the righteousness of God. He reasoned accurately and walked sinlessly. Eve shared in the bliss of being precisely in the image of God while living in Paradise. This is the pristine meaning of being made in God's image reflected when the Westminster Confession defines it as being 'endued with knowledge, righteousness, and true holiness, after his own image'.[4]

What happened to the image in the Fall?

The first couple's unblemished state was short-lived, and as we've already noticed, the perfect image of God in them was distorted but not destroyed. The Bible lets us know this when it tells us man is still in God's image after the Fall. Following the flood God made a covenant with Noah (Gen. 9:6) which makes clear that shedding the blood of another human is sinful. Why? '...for in the image of God has God made man'. Despite our fallenness, all persons still share in the image of God in such a way as to make every human life valuable. This is the reason Christians defend human life. Using the same argument, James sees cursing others as evil because men 'have been made in God's likeness' (James 3:9). Scripture again teaches that good treatment of others follows from their being made in God's image. We understand, then, that children (and all other humans) have intrinsic value because they share in the image of God. Christians are to recognize this and consequently value all persons.

Though the image remains, it isn't what it used to be. John Calvin states this plainly, 'Even though we grant that God's image was not totally annihilated and destroyed in him [Adam], yet it was so corrupted that whatever remains is frightful deformity.'[5] Accurate knowledge and holiness no longer characterize man in his sinful state. God's pronouncement that man was 'very good' in Genesis 1:31 changes after sin to the description of Genesis 6:5: 'The LORD saw how great man's wickedness on the earth had become, and that every inclination of the thoughts of his heart was only evil all the time.' We now bear God's image, but it is only a vague shadow of what it originally was.

Let's see how each of the aspects of the image changed after Adam's sin. Man no longer enjoys the pure knowledge and accurate reasoning of his pristine state, yet some aspects of these persist. Theologian Carl Henry tells us that Augustine maintained that the remnants of the intellectual image included 'the laws of logic, the immediate consciousness of self-existence, the truths of mathematics, and the moral truth that one ought to seek wisdom.'[6]

Let's look more closely at each of these.

The laws of logic are still around and give us our most basic form of reasoning. If an argument disobeys these laws, then it isn't acceptable (though fallen persons frequently fail to discern irrational arguments). In Christian education circles, there is increasing interest in making logic a part of children's curriculum to help them sort truth from error. Interestingly, this in itself represents a break from the excessively practical education that marks our time and a return to the standards of instruction which have guided much of Western history.

Secondly, humans alone among the earthly creatures have an awareness of ourselves as individuals. This is seen, for example, in the simple but startling notion that only humans realize that they will die some day. An awareness of our mortality is an interesting part of the image, because had Adam not sinned, we would not be subject to death.

Next, most everyone generally agrees with mathematical truths without question. Two plus two equals four anywhere you go (though I know a few children who would even argue this just for the fun of it!).

Finally, secular as well as Christian authorities hold the value of wisdom. Education is encouraged in almost all circles of modern thinking, even to the point that many humanists believe that more education alone will solve all our problems. While we agree with education as a worthwhile venture, it alone will not compensate for the sin that is in us, and can even be used to divert children from true paths of wisdom since we are fallen. We understand, then, that certain intellectual functions persist since the Garden of Eden, but these are often misused and misguided.

Remnants of the moral aspect of the image of God also remain in sinful humans. Paul teaches us in Romans 1:18–20 and 2:15 that fallen humans still have the law written on their hearts, specifically in their consciences. There are similar basic moral values throughout various cultures, many of these resembling the second table (the fifth through the tenth) of the Ten Commandments fairly well. Thus, while the image of God within us tells us there is law, our fallenness pushes us to rebel against it. This leaves people torn between some impulse to do right and another to do wrong. Remember the old cartoons that would picture an 'angel' and 'devil' appearing on either side of the character's head, one urging good and the other bad behaviour? This shows a surprisingly good insight into our conflicting spiritual nature, though we need not invoke angels and devils to account for it.

I often point out to parents the power of this sense of what is right by having them observe how fiercely teenagers will fight against something they see as 'unfair', for this is an emotional response to moral injury (even though their ideas of what is 'fair' often make little sense, showing the distortion of reason and morality in humans following Adam's sin).

What this means for children

This has been rather technical, so we would do well to consider the implications of the image of God for our ministry to children.

Intellectual abilities are cultivated naturally by parents around the world. We expectantly await the first words of our infants and try to hasten the day they can read and write. Motivated children eagerly learn all kinds of things, so we now know that our natural tendency toward learning is attributable to our being made in the image of God. But there is more. The fallen nature of the image warns us that care should be taken in teaching children. Nothing here suggests that children are eager only to learn what is right. It seems they are more often enthusiastic about learning things that aren't good for them. Observe how children are motivated to master violent video games while they are often apathetic about memory verses. A task of Christian ministry to children, whether by parents, teachers, or clergy, is to teach them a Christian world and life view, not just the 'facts'. This also implies we must guard our little ones from learning things that fuel their sinful natures.

Proverbs repeatedly points to the value of wisdom and the role of parents in passing it on. As modern parents we must understand we can't pass on what we don't have. It is essential that Christians be active in 'continuing education' for themselves, studying the Bible, Christian books, and other fields so we develop a well-informed Christian world view. Then, we must be aggressive in teaching our children a Christian framework that integrates what they know. We'll dig deeper into this in Chapter 6.

Most parents have not thought much about the moral nature of children or its being part of the image of God, but this has not hindered us from diligent efforts to teach children right and wrong through instruction and correction. Understanding the spiritual roots of our moral tendencies gives us greater appreciation for the abilities of children to learn to tell right from wrong. This reminds adults working with children of their responsibility to teach them the truth about what is right, educating them in the biblical standards of morality and preparing them to challenge the misguided ideas of right prevalent in the world around us.

The moral image is even evident is some way to the secular culture as it believes something is 'out of order' with criminals who lack any conscience or moral feeling. But humanists miss the point when they assume that because we all have some sense of what is right, we will generally follow it. They fail to appreciate how distorted our sense of morality is because of sin. Even as Christians, our experience teaches us that we, like Paul in Romans 7:21–3, have powerful impulses to do wrong, even when we know what is right and want to do it. This leads to the need for correction and discipline, a topic we'll explore in Chapter 7.

To summarize, we have learned that an understanding of the image of God gives us much insight into children, showing us that they have an inclination to learn and to have a 'conscience' about right and wrong. Both of these are distorted due to the sinful nature we share since Adam's transgression. Our learning is plagued by errors in logic and tendencies to see things as we wish instead of as they are. We are still moral beings, but left to ourselves we define what is right by our own standards and not the objective standards of the Bible. The remnants of God's image give us positive material with which to work as we minister to children, but remind us how careful we must be to guide these little ones into the truth.

Conceived in Sin

Children are quite a paradox. At times they are incredibly cute. Witness the 'oohs' and 'aahs' of well-wishers peering into the newborn's nursery, or the delightful photos of gleefully playing children that grace television ads and magazine articles. On the other hand, few things in life are as exasperating as children. Most parents recall the sleepless nights that followed the 'oohs' and 'aahs', and how that beautiful baby seemed quite a nuisance as she refused comfort from her red-eyed, exhausted mum and dad. That's not to mention the terrible heartache many parents endure as they see their teenagers turn against the values they have laboured to pass on to them. Cute or not, children are inclined to self-centredness and sin. I have never discovered a parenting book that explained to fathers and mothers how to help their perfectly good children develop some sense of mischief.

We are not left to decide for ourselves whether children are inclined toward good or evil by nature. The Word of God has clearly spoken, but it is a message we are woefully reluctant to hear. Let the reader beware. Any notions you carry about the innate goodness of children, no matter how precious they are, do not find support in the Bible. The teaching of Scripture challenges our culture's optimistic view that children are born morally good. We must lay aside any such false preconceptions we have developed on our own lest we build our families on sand. Rather, we must build our understanding of the nature of children on the rock of God's Word. Our beliefs about the spiritual nature of children have staggering implications for our ministry to them, so let us carefully search for biblical answers.

We begin by surveying some of the key texts about our standing before God at birth.

One of the clearest verses is Psalm 51:5 where David confesses, 'Surely I have been a sinner from birth, sinful from the time my mother conceived me.' Little doubt is left that David, inspired by God, views himself to have been sinful from conception on. We can see the logic behind this in the words of Job (14:4), 'Who can bring what is pure from the impure? No-one!' If adults are sinful, then it makes no sense that they could produce sinless offspring, for any tree brings forth fruit only after its own kind. The exception to this, of course, is the virgin birth of Christ who was born of Mary but who had no earthly father.

Other references support David's position that we are sinful from conception. Eliphaz, Job's friend, comments, 'What is man that he could be pure, or one born of woman, that he could be righteous?' (Job 15:14). Psalm 58 is also attributed to David, and in verse 3 he observes, 'Even from birth the wicked go astray; from the womb they are wayward and speak lies.' Lest one try to say this applies only to the wicked, remember these words are from the same man who described himself in Psalm 51 as sinful since conception. Despite his failures, David assuredly was a man of God. In Ephesians 2:3, Paul teaches that we are 'by nature objects of wrath'. God would be unjust if he targeted his wrath at creatures that are by nature innocent, so we must conclude that we are sinful from the start.

How can this be? Paul answers this urgent question in the primary text on the topic, Romans 5:12–19. This is crucial enough to merit quoting in full.

Therefore, just as sin entered the world through one man, and death through sin, and in this way death came to all men, because all sinned—for before the law was given, sin was in the world. But sin is not taken into account when there is no law. Nevertheless, death reigned from the time of Adam to the time of Moses, even over those who did not sin by breaking a command, as did Adam, who was a pattern of the one to come.

But the gift is not like the trespass. For if the many died by the trespass of the one man, how much more did God's grace and the gift that came by the grace of the one man, Jesus Christ, overflow to the many! Again, the gift of God is not like the result of the one man's sin: The judgment followed one sin and brought condemnation, but the gift followed many trespasses and brought justification. For if, by the trespass of the one man, death reigned through that one man, how much more will those who receive God's abundant provision of grace and of the gift of righteousness reign in life through the one man, Jesus Christ.

Consequently, just as the result of one trespass was condemnation for all men, so also the result of one act of righteousness was justification that brings life for all men. For just as through the disobedience of the one man the many were made sinners, so also through the obedience of the one man the many will be made righteous.

Surely there is more to discuss in this passage than our present task allows, so allow me to draw out a few points that will help us understand the spiritual nature of children.

Sin causes death (Rom. 5:12). Adam would still be around if he had not sinned. Since he did, he must pay the price and that is death (Gen. 2:17; Ezek. 18:4, 20; Rom. 6:23). No sin, no death. If there is death, there must be sin.

All people die, so all are sinful (Rom. 5:12). After Adam sinned, he brought forth offspring made in his image, not God's (Gen. 5:3). As a result, all people are sinful and die, some infants and children included. We know that horrible diseases like aids can be passed to the infant from the mother even though the infant has done nothing personally to deserve it. Sin also is passed from parent to child.

Sin is a condition, not just specific acts (Eph. 2:1–3; Gal. 5:19–21). If I can borrow again from our aids illustration, one can be infected with hiv without manifesting the symptoms for some time. The symptoms merely reveal the disease that is already present. So it is with sin: we are born in it, and the individual acts of wrongdoing serve to remind us of the disease within us. This comparison fails when we remember we are spiritually dead in our sins (Eph. 2:1). Romans 5:14 teaches us that those who lived without a law to tell them specifically what was right and wrong still died. Why? Because sin is more than breaking rules willfully; it is a condition of the heart.

Sin is imputed to all people (Rom. 5:18). This statement summarizes much of our text. To impute is to lay something to someone's account. The sin of Adam is laid to our account as his offspring, and this is why we are sinful before we commit specific acts of sin, and why David could claim to be conceived in sin. Does this seem unfair? Thank God it is not, for the same principle lies behind our salvation. Our sins are forgiven by imputation: God held Jesus accountable for our actions and punished him in our stead. Then, as we see clearly in Romans 5, God takes the righteousness of Christ and imputes it to us. If we cannot be held accountable for what someone else does, then the plan of salvation falls apart.

Therefore, infants are conceived in sin. The basic point in all of this is that infants are sinful from the start because the sin of Adam is imputed to them (placed to their account) since they are born of sinful parents. The formal name for this is *original sin*. This doesn't just mean the sin of Adam, but it refers to the sinful nature in all of us because we are related to Adam. This guilt may come from Adam, but in God's eyes it is justly ours. Proof of this is seen in the deaths of infants and children. If children were guiltless, God would be unfair to let them die. Since infants are subject to death, we admit they are indeed conceived in sin, just as David said.

What does this mean for us? It means young children may be naïve, but they are certainly not innocent. Original sin implies that all people are totally depraved, meaning that every part of their being is infected by sin. Even though children may have impulses to do good, these are still compromised by motives other than to please God (for example, to avoid a punishment). This is developed in passages such as John 5:42, Romans 7:18; 8:7–8, Ephesians 4:18 and Titus 1:15. Original sin also explains why every child who lives long enough will show their sinful nature by doing wrong.

The other aspect of original sin is total inability. This means we are ultimately unable to please God in our own power. Jesus taught this when he proclaimed that 'No-one can come to me unless the Father who sent me draws him' (John 6:44). Jesus also would have us understand that 'apart from me you can do nothing' (John 15:5). Paul further demonstrates this truth in Romans 8:7–8 by saying, 'the sinful mind is hostile to God. It does not submit to God's law, nor can it do so. Those controlled by the sinful nature cannot please God.' Spiritually dead persons can do nothing to better their estate. As for our children, God must intervene in their lives to change their natures if they are to be free from sin.

Lessons from the doctrine of original sin

Understanding these truths is hard work, but laying a foundation is often the dirtiest part of building a house. So it is in preparing to minister biblically to children. Now, let's consider the practical aspects of what we have learned.

First, children are born in sin. The Bible does not leave any room for the idea that children are naturally inclined toward good. Though remnants of the image leave children with a conscience, it can readily be led away from the truth of God's law. Moreover, being naturally sinful, we are unable to fulfil the law anyway. This is why the cross is essential.

Because they are born in sin, some children die in infancy. Being sinful in their nature, God is just to execute the penalty of death upon them. Do these little ones have a chance for heaven? Stay tuned for our next chapter.

Children need to be taught the need for God's saving grace. Discipline has a major place in the life of a child, but spankings and other punishments will not get them to heaven. Those ministering to children as parents or in other roles must teach children of their sinfulness. Jonathan Edwards, the Puritan pastor and theologian, referred to children as 'little vipers' to make clear the potency of original sin. We may not use language quite that graphic, but we must not teach 'self-esteem' in such a way that children fail to see their sinfulness before God and their need for salvation. Since salvation is of God's grace, diligent prayers are needed for the children under our charge.

Children will always struggle with concupiscence. This may be a new term for many, and it can be defined as the 'wrongful inclination of the sinner which characterizes his nature and leads to sinful acts'.[7] This term was a favourite of Augustine, and described the ongoing yearning to do wrong that persists even after we are saved. It might be called 'lust' or 'inordinate desires' in our day, but it suggests that our sinful nature still tempts us. For parents, this means that our children, even if they are clearly Christians, will battle with tendencies toward wrong (just like their parents!) and will need ongoing discipline and direction. Our discipline may serve like a fence to contain an untamed animal, but it does not take away the animal's impulses to break free. It is the task of God to 'tame' the 'wildness' of our little ones while we attempt to restrain their impulses and garner their cooperation in the struggle. By educating children about their sinful nature, we help them realize the struggle they face. Discipline alone will not exterminate concupiscence, so we must prepare our little ones for the lifelong battle against sin, one which we as adults share.

But be careful! Building on the notion of original sin, there are some Christians who teach that the selfish impulses of children should be dealt with from the start. They advocate not responding to the hungry cries of newborns except at certain times to teach them who is boss from the start. Sadly, this thinking fails to understand that such cries from very young babies are vital because, unless someone responds, they will die in their helplessness. The first lesson babies need to learn is that there is someone there for them when they are in distress, forming in them a sense of trust and attachment. As the baby grows, crying may become manipulative and can then be dealt with from the context of the parent-child relationship without the risk of trauma. Selfishness is wrong, but it is not to be confused with genuine need and a desire for security.

We now have some ideas about what the Bible teaches about the nature of children. Even sin did not destroy the image of God in its entirety, leaving our little ones with desires and abilities to learn, and moral leanings which can be shaped for good or ill. Children are conceived and born in sin, subject to its penalty of death like all of us. We know that we must prayerfully seek God's saving grace for their lives and His guidance in preparing them for the battle against sin, teaching them about their sinful nature and 'concupiscence'. Discipline is required as we try to shape and restrain the behaviour of our little ones, but ultimately God must change their hearts. The spiritual tasks of prayer and teaching are more decisive for spiritual victory than simply knowing how to punish children better. Viewed in the light of their spiritual nature, ministry to children is more of a challenge. Yet, it is a most honourable and vital work when undertaken with an absolute dependence on God's grace.

4

HOW AND WHEN
CAN CHILDREN BE SAVED?

*It's strange to know that she is surely at peace. And that she
is well off there, very well off, and yet to grieve so much!*
(Martin Luther, on the death of his daughter, Magdalene)

It wasn't strange in Luther's day to have children die. This did
not prevent the great reformer from feeling intense sorrow for
his beloved Magdalene who was taken from him during her
fourteenth year. His loss was comforted by the fact that he had
confidence that his daughter died as a Christian, though yet
a child.

Death has a way of clarifying our priorities. Though we pray
that our Father would leave our children with us to enjoy, the
thought of their eternal fate puts all we do as parents and those
who work with and care for children in perspective. We are easily
caught up in secondary objectives in our ministry to children. We
exert great energy to provide the best educational opportunities
for our little ones, even if we have to suffer financially in
the process. We provide music lessons, soccer camps, and
a host of other enriching activities to encourage them toward
well-rounded lives. We take care to clothe our children well and
teach them manners, striving to give them the best chance at

social survival. We indulge too many of their wishes, failing to resist the temptations of their requests as we are so eager to see them happy.

As Christians, however, we would trade all of these secondary goals for the most important one, to share with Luther the assurance that our children are also God's children, citizens of the kingdom of heaven. When our children meet eternity, whether sooner or later, all else is for naught if they don't know Jesus as their Saviour.

Taking this one step further, as followers of Christ, we also long for our children to be servants of the kingdom of God who grow in holiness and ministry to others. We hope that our 'well-done' is an echo of the 'well-done' of our children's heavenly Father. I believe most Christians who nurture children as parents or in other capacities would agree with the following goal for their work: To see our children cling to faith in Christ and invest their lives, now and for eternity, glorifying and enjoying God. Goals such as education, 'success' in this life, enrichment, social relationships, and material security all must be subordinate to this great objective for our children. It is indeed the focus of this book to set this goal before us and to lead us into concerted efforts to achieve it in our homes and churches.

The first requirement of this goal is that our children be believers in the saving work of Christ. Let us consider whether children need to be saved, and if so, how it is accomplished.

Do children need to be saved? The problem of infant death.

At first glance, this might seem to be a rather unnecessary question on which to spend time. Of course children need to be saved: 'for all have sinned and fall short of the glory of God' (Rom. 3:23). But wait a second. What about very young children and infants? The problem is that some children die while very young, and what is their eternal fate? We have little problem with the need for adults to profess faith in Christ before dying, but what of those who cannot as yet speak or understand the need for a Saviour? Explaining this will expose what we really believe about the need for salvation.

The death of young children and infants has long been a theological puzzle. It forces us to look at our view of sin and the way God administers saving grace. Let's look at a few of the opinions Christians offer about the fate of children dying in infancy.

THE SOLUTION OF INNOCENCE

Many Christians who have given this matter little thought may answer that those who die in infancy go to heaven because they are innocent. God does not see them as guilty of sin. This view dates back at least to the time of the heretic Pelagius who in the early fifth century was puzzled by dying infants. If the 'wages of sin is death', then infants who die are guilty of sin from the start and that would argue against man's ability to fulfil God's requirements for righteousness on his own (you see why he was considered a heretic!). Pelagius decided that death was part of being human even before Adam sinned, and thus it is not a punishment for sin.

That sounds rather strange to us today, as it should. Yet, some unwittingly argue the same way about children. These folks say that, though children die, they are really innocent and thus merit heaven by virtue of being sinless. Usually those of this persuasion think that sin is only a conscious act of disobedience, something of which a baby is incapable. When infants die, the advocates of the innocence view are comforted in the belief that all such infants go to heaven.

There are two problems with this. First, why do infants die in this case? We are back to Pelagius where death is not a consequence of sin. If the believers in the natural innocence of children don't want to deny death as a consequence of sin, they may try to set the occurrence of death free from God's control. Here the idea is that God is not involved when infants die. Many Christians today choose this view as a way of defending God against being blamed for tragic deaths of little children. However, it is too high a price to remove control from God, for then he is no longer sovereign and we have to wonder how many other things are outside of his control. Besides, we've already seen that the Bible is fairly clear that we are sinners from conception. As we read in Psalm 14:3, 'there is no-one who does good, not even one'.

The second problem with this view is that it disagrees with Jesus' statement in John 14:6, 'I am the way and the truth and the life. No-one comes to the Father except through me.' If dying infants deserve heaven because they are innocent, they reach heaven without needing Christ. We would then have two ways to glory instead of one.

The problem here is that sin is wrongly defined as individual acts only, not as a state. We sin because we have sinful hearts. Even when we are not engaged in a specific sinful act, sin remains in us. R. A. Webb aptly summarizes how this applies to our discussion: 'Infants…are not absolutely, but only relatively innocent. From one kind of sin they are free; from another kind they are not. They are free from "actual sin", but they are not free from "original sin".'

THE SOLUTION OF THE AGE OF ACCOUNTABILITY

This is similar to the innocence view in some ways, but is different enough to look at separately. Advocates of this view hold to a doctrine of original sin, but engineer a way to get dying children to heaven anyway.

The traditional Catholic view, tracing its roots to Augustine, is that baptism washes away original sin, leaving the child in a condition of moral ignorance until he is able to commit actual sin. To cover those infants who died without being baptized, the notion of 'limbo' was developed, this being the place of 'natural happiness' for these little ones.

A comparable view is held by many who claim that original sin may incline the person to sin, and may even mean that those living long enough will inevitably sin, but that God does not hold young children accountable for their sins. Unlike the Catholics, these believers do not offer much solution for original sin other than seeing it as an impulse and not really sin. We are only obligated to do as well as our ability lets us. Since infants are not able to understand sin, they are relieved of responsibility and can go to heaven if they die. This means that original sin is not eternally punishable, and they enter heaven by virtue of not being guilty of sin for which they are accountable.

This position has as a correlate the idea of an age of account-ability. In this, the child reaches some uncertain age (we must try to judge it from when we think the child is capable of wilful wrongdoing) at which he or she becomes responsible for his or her sin because he or she knows better. So, technically a child could tell a lie one week and not be accountable, but then be worthy of condemnation for the same lie the following week if he or she reached the age of accountability in the meantime. The basis for this seems to come from modern legal thinking which might hold one unaccountable for crimes if one were not capable of responsible action (due to insanity, for example). In God's court, sin is falling short of his glory, regardless of how capable we are.

The age of accountability position still leaves us with two ways to heaven as infants gain entry when found not guilty by reason of inability. This view shortchanges the biblical teaching on original sin and the broader biblical view of sin as expressed in the *Westminster Shorter Catechism* (Question 14): 'Sin is any want of conformity unto, or transgression of, the law of God.' Certainly we want hope for infants who die, but this view does too much damage to the truth of Scripture to be acceptable.

THE SENTIMENTAL SOLUTION

Here is a stepchild of liberal theology. If we accept the liberal argument that 'God is love' is the total description of the Deity, and view him as the Father of all persons, not just his redeemed ones, then we will conclude that God would never allow his infant children to go to hell. Of course, this would not explain why a child should die, as this would be 'unloving' in their view. Most likely the advocates of sentimentality must disengage God from the death of infants altogether to acquit him of any charges of cruelty. Such an impotent god who is tolerant of sin is simply not the God of the Bible. While God is love, he is also holy. While he is Father to his people, he is merely Creator to everyone else. (Recall our discussion of adoption earlier.)

GOD'S SOVEREIGN SOLUTION

In reviewing the previous three positions, we have seen that all require us to compromise something of the nature of God. As badly as we wish to find hope for children dying in infancy, we cannot alter the character of God to meet our needs. Let us lay down three foundations to prepare for a more palatable solution to the problem.

Original sin. As we saw in Chapter 3, all children are conceived in the blight of original sin. Sin brings death, and death spreads to all people (Rom. 5:12). Original sin explains why infants die, but this blight must be cleansed for them to enter heaven.

Jesus blesses the children. The Gospels depict Jesus blessing children who were brought to him by their parents (Matt. 19:13–15; Mark 10:13–16; Luke 18:15–17), saying the kingdom of heaven belongs to such as these. There undoubtedly is a metaphorical interpretation of this, but we cannot overlook the literal one. Jesus blessed children brought by their parents and implied they were of the kingdom of God, even though nothing is said of the children doing anything themselves.

The necessity of regeneration. Jesus flatly stated to Nicodemus, 'You must be born again' (John 3:7). If we are dead in our sins (e.g. Eph. 2:1), then we must be made alive again, or regenerated. In Reformed thought, regeneration precedes faith, faith being impossible for the dead person. God is seen as the Author and Initiator of regeneration. This is seen is places such as Genesis 12 where God calls Abram and Acts 9 where Saul is suddenly called by God. If adult faith is of divine origin, then, as Geoffrey Bromiley rightly remarks, 'infant faith in Christ cannot be regarded as a divine impossibility.'[2]

These facts will be important because the Bible is strangely quiet on the fate of those who die in infancy. The only reference that is directly applicable is David's comment about his recently deceased son (2 Sam. 12:23), 'I will go to him, but he will not return to me.' This does not give us a clear statement on our subject at all. However, it certainly leaves us with an optimistic note that David would see his son again, though his son was only a few days old when he passed away. Given that David was a man of God (though not at his best at the time of this story!), it is safe to assume that David believed his son was with God in heaven. (Some say that he would have figured his son was in 'sheol' or the grave. This would not explain the apparent intent of the statement to comfort David.) So, the only distinct reference in the Bible to a child dying in infancy gives suggestion that the child went to be with the Lord.

Since we then have hope, what is its basis? I believe it is in the doctrine of election. We see a hint of this when Jesus blesses the children brought by their parents, and another in the doctrine of regeneration. Clearer evidence comes from Romans 8:29–30 where the gospel sequence goes: foreknowledge, predestination, calling, justification and glorification. Each of these steps has God as its Author, meaning that he could choose to effect these on infants if he pleased. The Bible describes some infants as being chosen from the womb, including Jacob (Rom. 9:11–13), Isaiah (Isa. 49:1, 5), Jeremiah (Jer. 1:5), Paul (Gal. 1:15), and David (Ps. 22:10). David is also described as trusting God at his mother's breasts (Ps. 22:9). Recall also John the Baptist's spiritual vitality even before birth (Luke 1:41). There seems adequate evidence to say God can manifest his election before birth.

Even so, if we are saved through faith, how are wordless infants to express it? Ephesians 2:8–9 gives the answer: it is a gift of God. If faith required verbal expression, then this is a work of ours. God can give wordless persons faith, even if they are still babes.

How many dying infants are saved?

This is a hotly debated issue with three basic options:

1. ALL CHILDREN DYING IN INFANCY ARE ELECT. This is the most optimistic view and the most widely held. However, there is no direct Scripture proof for it except to argue that the only example of a child dying in infancy whose fate is mentioned leads us to believe he was elect. If this is true, the implications are staggering as one considers the high infant mortality rate throughout history. Spurgeon would then be right in stating of heaven, 'It is rather a kingdom of children than of men.'[3]

2. ALL CHILDREN OF TRUE BELIEVERS ARE ELECT IF THEY DIE IN INFANCY. This is the position of the Synod of Dort and may include Calvin among its supporters. This holds

that the covenant promise (to be discussed later in this chapter) applies to all children of believers, though it may be forfeited if they are unfaithful to the covenant as they mature. Calvin avoids the notion of losing one's salvation by saying that God must add a spirit of regeneration to the covenant promise for it to be effective.[4]

3. SOME CHILDREN, PRIMARILY OF BELIEVING PARENTS, ARE SAVED. *The Westminster Confession of Faith* carefully states (Ch. 10, Section III), 'Elect infants, dying in infancy, are regenerated and saved by Christ through the Spirit.' This is the most judicious position given our lack of biblical data. It assumes God's ability to choose infants, and assumes most of them will come from the covenant family, but leaves room for exceptions.[5]

We therefore find comfort in God's gracious ability to regenerate infants and give them wordless faith so that they, too, can be heirs of heaven. We have special cause to be optimistic when children of believers die because of God's covenant promises, though it may well be that God claims all dying infants as his own. It is certainly his to choose to do so.

Our study of the fate of children dying in infancy underscores the fact that all children are born sinners and need to be saved. We turn now to consider the more usual situation of children who grow in years, and how they come to faith.

How do our children become Christians?

There is, of course, the simple answer to this: they believe that Jesus died on the cross to save them from their sins, just like anyone else. But this fails to deal with the particular issues relating to children, such as does baptism save? Is a specific, memorable conversion necessary? Are those with Christian parents advantaged in any way? Our search for answers to these and similar questions is complicated by the fact that the Bible does not directly answer these questions, nor does it give a clear example of a child accepting Christ. Yet, these matters are very important and weigh heavily on the hearts of parents and others that minister to children. We need to make an effort to provide some answers, even if they must be submitted rather humbly in light of the limited scriptural teaching about the salvation of children.

We will begin by looking briefly at several practices that have been used with regard to the faith of children. We will linger a little more on the last section, as I believe it offers us the most fully biblical view.

BORN AGAIN BY BAPTISM

This is more formally called 'baptismal regeneration' and admittedly it is the model with the most advocates in church history. We met Augustine earlier, and he was an early champion of the idea that original sin is washed away when infants are baptized. He also added that it brought saving grace to the recipients, that grace being in the sacrament itself. This became the standard position of the Roman Catholic Church and has continued until our day. Some of the Protestant churches spawned in the Reformation carry similar beliefs into their practice of infant baptism, including those who follow Luther himself.

There are at least two problems with this view. If faith is produced by an outward act, then that faith is not wholly free of works. The behaviour of the parents and the act of the minister play roles in salvation. It is no longer purely of grace as Paul teaches in Ephesians 2:8–9. Imagine the terror of many parents during history who, despite their faith, desperately waited for the arrival of a priest to administer the sacrament; their dying child's eternal destiny lying in the balance.

The sign of baptism cannot be equated with the grace it signifies. Consider the Old Testament practice of circumcision. Most who received it did not go on to exhibit the faith of Abraham. Paul explains in Romans 2:28–9: 'A man is not a Jew if he is only one outwardly, nor is circumcision merely outward and physical. No, a man is a Jew if he is one inwardly; and circumcision is circumcision of the heart, by the Spirit, not by the written code.' So, while baptism may represent grace, we cannot be certain that the recipient is or will be a believer.

The second problem with the belief that baptism confers salvation is the major problem of the numbers of persons baptized as infants but who go on to deny the faith and to live godless lives. This leaves us with a terribly shallow view of what it is to be a Christian. This problem can also be handled by claiming that the salvation received at baptism can be lost, but then we are deprived of the assurance offered in texts such as John 10:28–9; Philippians 1:6; 1 Peter 1:5; 2 Peter 1:10 and 1 John 3:9. It appears that assuming a child is saved because he or she was baptized as an infant is inconsistent with the teaching of the Bible.

CONFIRMATION

This practice evolved as a way of supplementing infant baptism, showing that the recipient made a conscious decision to profess the faith received at baptism for themselves. That is why it is called confirmation; it is a confirming of something previously determined (as when we get a confirmation of a hotel reservation). Confirmation achieved the status of sacrament in Roman Catholic circles but is seen merely as a 'rite' in Protestant arenas where it is practised.

Confirmation is positive in its reflection of the need for individuals to express ownership of their faith when they are old enough to understand it. This is especially true in light of the poor record of many baptized as infants. It is also a worthy practice in that it establishes a way for children raised in a church to enter it formally, offering a rite of passage missing in modern times. Still, confirmation acts only as a form of 'quality control' and cannot be seen as saving anyone by itself.

PERSONAL DECISIONS FOR CHRIST

Here is the most common view of the salvation of children in evangelical circles today. Its most common form runs like this. The child grows to reach an age of accountability and inevitably sins. The child realizes his sinfulness and makes a personal decision to repent of his sins while accepting by faith that Jesus paid for his sins on the cross. This is often during the invitation at a church service, or is made public if it occurred in private.

Such an arrangement has much to commend it. Certainly the New Testament shows persons being converted after hearing the gospel, especially in the Book of Acts. Such sudden conversions fit with the idea of the 'turning' of repentance or the 'new birth' of regeneration. They also provide a definite event to point back to when a person doubts his or her faith in later years.

There is a certain theology to this, of course. Such views most often stress the individual's choice about salvation and the need for faith to occur before regeneration. Strangely, many who hold to this insist one cannot lose his or her salvation after such an event, even if he or she choose to desert the faith. In that sense it is a twist on freedom of the will in that one can will to be saved but loses freedom after that. Persons who hold to such a view often disapprove of infant baptism because of the inability of infants to decide for themselves and, as we have mentioned, the poor record of some who were baptized.

While I will not argue that sudden conversions do occur and can be genuine, even in the lives of children, there are important problems with this view. First is the problem of setting an age at which conversion can occur. In church history children were generally not admitted to full membership in the church until they reached ten or more years of age. Conversions are reported at ages as young as four. While certain developmental differences are to be expected, there are questions as to how much of the nature of salvation must a child understand before making such a major decision. Children raised in churches holding to this view know what is expected of them and are encouraged to make a profession of faith. The pressure applied to young children can range from the natural desires to please one's parents to the terrifying threats of a fiery evangelist. Children who make decisions might easily do so for questionable motives.

Many churches believe that such conversions are God's only way of bringing little ones to himself yet admit that care must be taken to determine the quality of the child's understanding and the nature of his motives. Little stress may be given in such child evangelism to informing the child of the challenges of the Christian life so that he or she can 'count the cost' (Luke 14:28–30) before making such a decision. Most often there is not a dramatic turning of a sinful life into a godly one, and later behaviour may not reflect a change of heart. In my work, I have talked with a number of burdened parents whose children had gone through the right steps but still did not seem to have a heart for God.

Other churches make this practice dangerous as they firmly stress that recollection of such an experience is the greatest evidence of salvation. This means that as these children grow they may take comfort in being Christians because they walked down the aisle at eight years of age, even if they show little or no interest in the things of God now. I can think of no place in Scripture where we are pointed to a past experience for assurance of our salvation. Present faith and a desire to follow Christ appear to be the best indicators of genuine faith (see, e.g., Matt. 7:19–20; Gal. 6:4; James 1:19–27; 2:14–26; 1 John 2:3; 3:18–19).

There is not a biblical example of a child coming to the faith by such a decision. Of course, the Book of Acts only covers the first generation of Christians and says little of how the faith passed on to the next generation. It does not say whether sudden conversions were the norm for the children of the first generation of Christ's followers. There is a similar problem in the conversionist view as it deprives Christian parents of any particular hopes for the salvation of their children. Scripture teaches that children have some relationship to the faith of their parents, and this will be considered as we turn to the covenant view of salvation of children.

CHILDREN OF THE COVENANT

The 'personal decision' model we have just examined has one assumption we did not mention: it assumes God views humans on an individual basis. The gospel is offered and individuals respond to it. Is this the case in Scripture? It doesn't seem to be.

Scripture suggests that God has voluntarily reached to man through covenants. He offered life to Adam and his posterity upon the condition of perfect obedience, this being the covenant of works. We know this didn't last long, but notice that Adam didn't act for himself alone; his offspring was affected. Following Adam's sin, God compassionately instituted a new covenant, this one of grace. In it, sinners are offered life based on the work of Christ and faith in him, Christ being the 'second Adam'. Specific covenants in Bible history work this out in more detail.

If you study the biblical texts telling of God's covenanting, you will be impressed by the fact that covenants are made with families rather than individuals, and children are included in these; Genesis 17:7 and Acts 2:39 being two of the clearest examples. God routinely deals with families in the Bible. Examples include his dealings with Noah (Gen. 6:17–18; 7:1), Lot (Gen. 19:12), Israel on the Passover (Exod. 12:21), the Law (Exod. 20:4–6), Korah's rebellion (Num. 16:25–33), and Paul's prayer for Onesiphorus' family (2 Tim. 1:16). Baptisms in the New Testament were frequently household baptisms (Acts 11:14; 16:15, 31–3; 18:8; 1 Cor. 1:16).[6]

In some sense, then, children are included with their parents when God makes covenants, and the covenant of grace is not an exception. This inclusion, according to 1 Corinthians 7:14, makes children of believers 'holy' in some sense. Children of believers stand in some special relation to the grace of God compared to those born to unbelievers. While this truth is clear from Scripture, what are its implications for the salvation of children? There are three major positions that we will survey.

CHILDREN OF BELIEVERS ARE UNDOUBTEDLY SAVED

Some hold that, by virtue of being born to a believer, children of the covenant are automatically saved. This was the view of early Puritans such as Richard Baxter. Their reasoning was supported by texts such as Matthew 18:14 ('In the same way your Father in heaven is not willing that any of these little ones should be lost') and 2 Timothy 2:19 ('The Lord knows those who are his'). Still, not all who hold this position leave themselves without an escape route as they argued that children of believers should take care to be sure of their salvation by examining their hearts.

A danger of this type of thinking is that it often maintains that parental faith is the key to ensuring the child's salvation. If the child of the covenant is not a Christian, it is for lack of faith on the part of the parents. Authors such as Andrew Murray and Edward N. Gross take this position, though they are careful to say that salvation is not by works. Still, this would not offer David a good explanation for Absalom, nor would it be very comforting to other faithful parents who do sometimes have rebellious children. This makes it difficult to explain God's very preferential treatment of Jacob as opposed to Esau, even though they were twins.

CHILDREN OF BELIEVERS ARE ASSUMED TO BE UNSAVED UNTIL THEY SHOW CLEAR PROOF TO THE CONTRARY

This was the view of America's foremost theologian, Jonathan Edwards, who was concerned about the unchristian behaviour of many who had been baptized. Edwards saw no promise that all the children of believers were elect and regenerate, and thus viewed them as a primary field for evangelism. He believed children could be Christians and exhibit piety, but not simply by birthright. Yet, Edwards seems to have reacted so strongly to the abuses of the ideas of the covenant that he lost sight of the promises to believing parents we reviewed earlier.

CHRISTIAN PARENTS HAVE REASON TO HOPE FOR THE SALVATION OF THEIR CHILDREN

While Scripture does not appear to offer parents a guarantee of their salvation, the nature of covenants seems to offer a great deal of hope. This position is probably best articulated by the great theologian John Calvin. Calvin believed in a 'common election' of a people by God, meaning he drew most of his children from a body of people of his choosing. In the Old Testament, he covenanted with Abraham, and Israel became the people from whom almost all believers originated. In the New Testament, there is not a national people, so the covenant promises flow from the members of the church. This fits with our experience that most Christians in church history were children of believers. Our offspring form the greatest source of the succeeding generation of Christians.

Calvin believed infants were renewed by the Spirit of God, but by a faith that grew with the capacity of their age until it was fully manifest.[7] There were exceptions, but Christian parents could live in a hopeful expectancy that their growing children would exhibit faith in Christ and lives that go with it.

The best understanding of the covenant blessing to children of believers is that there is reason for parents to hope for and anticipate the salvation of their children though there is no room for complacency nor taking this hope for granted. Parents may see faith given to their children in infancy mature and blossom, leading to a clear profession and behaviour consistent with it. Others may see their children make a more specific decision to follow Christ. The manner is not as important as the impact, with the best evidence of belief being a life marked by love for God and a longing to follow in his ways. In this regard, age is not really an issue.

A token for children

We have now come full circle to answer the questions that began our chapter. Children are born in sin and are appropriate objects of God's wrath unless he intervenes. When infants or young children die, we have hope that they go to be with the Lord. As our children grow, we also hope that they are God's. Whether this is seen in a faith that grows with the child, or is manifest in a specific experience, the assurance comes from an ongoing love for and obedience to the living God. We now understand more of Luther's hope for his departed daughter.

We close this chapter with an account of young faith related in *A Token for Children*, stories of the lives of young children of faith related by Puritans James Janeway and Cotton Mather. Many of these children died in infancy, and their stories were preserved to provide a challenge to future generations. After our efforts to understand the faith of children, let us consider an example of what it can look like as we learn of a boy who died at the age of twelve:

> Charles Bridgman had no sooner learned to speak than he took himself to pray. He was very prone to learn the things of God. He would sometimes be teaching them their duty who waited upon him. He learned by heart many good things before he was well fit to go to school. And when he was sent to school, he carried it so that all who observed him either did or might admire him. O the sweet nature, the good disposition, the sincere religion, which was in him!
> ...[After falling ill] he inquired how his soul might be saved. The answer being made, 'by the applying of Christ's merits by faith,' he was pleased with the answer, and was ready to give any one who should desire it an account of his hope.

...The last words he spoke were exactly these, 'Pray, pray, pray, nay, yet pray. And the more prayers, the better all prospers. God is the best Physician. Into Thy hands I commend my spirit. O Lord Jesus, receive my soul! Now I close my eyes. Forgive me, father, mother, brother, sister, all the world. Now I am well, my pain is almost gone, my joy is at hand. Lord, have mercy on me. O Lord, receive my soul unto Thee!'[8]

CULTIVATING GODLY CHILDREN:
WHAT'S A PARENT TO DO?

'*Do not exasperate your children; instead, bring them up in the training and instruction of the Lord*' (Ephesians 6:4)

'*Families ... should be nurseries for heaven*' (Samuel Davies)

'*Only as genuine Christian holiness, and Christlike love are expressed in the life of a parent, can the child have the opportunity to inherit the flame and not the ashes*' (Stephen G. Green)

I am not much of a gardener, though I tried a few times before I realized it. My idea of starting a garden is to go to the local garden centre, buy some seeds, stick them in the ground, and wait a few weeks. The seeds should do their job and produce vegetables for us to enjoy (though according to my daughter, 'enjoy' and 'vegetables' should not be used in the same sentence!).

Those readers who know anything of the ways of gardening can readily list the reasons I failed. I've heard a few of them myself. You have to use good soil that gets adequate sunlight. If it isn't good enough, you add fertilizers to improve it. You have to plant the seeds with care, not too deep and not too shallow. They have to be watered and fertilized, neither over or underdoing these.

As the plants grow, all this must be continued while you also pull the weeds that are eager to steal the nutrients and sun from your prize vegetables. The list goes on, but the point is clear: I shouldn't expect success if I don't put continual care into my plants as they mature.

You may guess where I'm heading with this. Children are like the garden: they need constant nurturing if they are to mature spiritually. The analogy is helpful also because the gardener can create all the conditions for life and growth, but the seed must do the rest. So it is with children. They must spiritually be made alive by God (regenerated) and his Spirit must work spiritual growth in them. None the less, it is the task of parents to provide an environment that is conducive to spiritual health in their children. In this chapter we will consider how we can 'garden' our children effectively.

The goal of parenting

Modern life is quite hectic and frazzled, and it is easy to slip into a reactive style where you spend all your days responding to crises. Parenting can be like this. We react to our children when they are demanding something or when they obviously need us, having little plan other than getting through the day. This frequently means we are acting without clear objectives.

Many parents who come to my office are caught in such a cycle. Their children are becoming too difficult to manage, so the parents seek help to control them. The goal is often simply to ease the task of raising children, and even this goal is not consciously in the minds of the parents.

In contrast, the gardener has a specific goal in mind, and this drives his behaviour throughout the process. All his efforts for his garden revolve around the goal of vegetables on the table. His efforts are focused and proactive. You see where this is going, too, don't you? Parenting, especially by Christians, should be directed toward a goal. Doubtlessly there are times when we simply have to react to crises, but overall our efforts should move toward an end, a 'product' we hope to enjoy some day.

Certainly, you may say, but what is the goal toward which parents are to work? Several ideas emerge from Scripture, but it does not explicitly state a goal for parenting. Drawing from the biblical evidence, I venture to propose the following goal for Christian parenting: to raise children through guidance and discipline to faith in Christ, so that they glorify him in every area of their lives, eventually passing the faith on to their children.

This goal will shape what I have to say throughout this book, so let me take a moment to make this clear.

We saw in the last chapter that an initial goal of Christian parents is to see their children come to faith, for the stakes here are eternal. This is essential, and is the hinge upon which the rest of our goal rests. Unbelievers cannot glorify God nor will they care to pass faith on to subsequent generations. To return to our metaphor, if the seed doesn't germinate, there's no plant to cultivate. The guidance and discipline we give to children is not simply to maintain order, but to move our little ones toward God.

Once our children profess faith, then the focus is on nurturing sanctification in their lives. Here we borrow from *The Westminster Shorter Catechism* which states that man's chief end is to glorify God, and to enjoy him for ever. This can cover a large area, but particularly it should include obedience from the heart, love to God and neighbour, genuine worship, and a grasp of all of life being lived for the furtherance of the Kingdom of God. Finally, our goal brings this full circle as our children mature. If indeed they come to live to the glory of God, it will be natural that they become godly parents to their children. This establishes an ongoing line of faithful believers, effectively perpetuating the church (at least from within itself) until Christ's return.

I want to stress again that, as with the seeds in our garden, spiritual life in our children is not our work. It is bestowed by God's grace. Ours is merely to provide an environment conducive to its growth. For, as with a garden, I believe that a godly environment is greatly used by God to strengthen and mature the faith he grants to his children.

A Word on Guarantees

Is there a 'money-back guarantee' that if you pursue this goal and follow the steps I am about to outline, your children will become Christians and live exemplary lives for our Lord? I wish I could say 'Yes', but I cannot.

The closest to a 'guarantee' verse in Scripture is the famous text of Proverbs 22:6: 'Train a child in the way he should go, and when he is old he will not turn from it.' This statement has long troubled me because it sounds like a certain deal. But you, too, probably know cases where parents have faithfully raised their children in the Word and prayed diligently for them only to see them rebel and stray from the fold. How are we to account for such exceptions? There are at least two ways of reconciling such experiences with Proverbs 22:6.

First, can any of us truly say we have trained our children totally and perfectly in the way they should go? While some come closer to this standard than others, we all undoubtedly fall short of it in some ways. The text, then, would be interpreted to say that as we move toward the standard of how we should train our children, the 'odds' of them staying on the right path increase.

Second, we may interpret this as a general principle that, although true, is not necessarily true in every single case. For example, it is true that smokers do not live as long as non-smokers do. However, that statement does not mean that every single non-smoker outlives every single smoker. Similarly, then, our verse would be taken to mean that those who raise their children in accordance with biblical wisdom will have children who do not depart from it, though not in every single case. This interpretation frankly makes me a little nervous, so I prefer the former.

A colleague shared another caveat that may provide encouragement to parents of teens. The term 'old' can be translated as 'grown'. This seems to leave room for a period of rebellion where the child departs from their training, returning to it once they are grown. This is often the case with teens that rebel against the faith for a period before returning to walk with God.

So, while Proverbs 22:6 encourages a confident expectation that efforts to train children properly will bear fruit, we must understand that none of us are perfect parents, and so will never train our children perfectly. We ultimately must still rely on God's grace for our children, and not on whether we feel we have lived according to a specific formula. Finally, we should be especially grateful for those cases where children come to know Christ and to walk faithfully with him despite not being trained in his ways by their parents. These are indeed special examples of God's grace.

The divine example

Since we aspire to raise our children to godliness, it is appropriate to consider the way that God himself performs his role as Parent. We saw in Chapter 2 that God is Creator to all men, but Father only to believers, having adopted them to be his children. By considering how he deals with his children, we gain insight into ways to nurture our own.

God demonstrates common parenting tendencies such as discipline (Heb. 12:7), using circumstances and consequences to teach us obedience and faithfulness. This can be exemplified by his dealings with David after his sin with Bathsheba. In a broader sense, the blessings and cursings associated with keeping or breaking the law in the Old Testament can be seen as a disciplinary system. Yet, God the Father also shows other parental qualities such as compassion (Ps. 103:13), and encouragement (1 Thess. 2:11). Our Heavenly Father is a loving Parent (Rom. 8:38–39; Pss. 63:3; 69:16) who is sensitive to the needs of his children (Matt. 6:8, 32). He frees us from worry by his faithful provision (Matt. 6:25–33) as we seek first his kingdom. He also offers his children fellowship (1 John 1:3), the joyous ongoing relationship cherished by the faithful.

An important point here is that God does not simply punish us when we err, but provides and cares for us, engendering in his children comfort and confidence. We are to revere him, but also to trust in his grace and mercy. Many times Christian parents seem to think disciplining their children is the most important thing they do as parents. But, as our brief look at God as Father shows us, such a narrow view of being a parent does not reflect God's approach to the task. God's standard for his children is not legalistic obedience, but hearts that love him, trust him, and are eager to please him. This occurs in the context of an intimate relationship. Our parenting should reflect his.

If we want to create a home that is conducive to godliness, we must learn more of God himself and how he cares for us. Christian parents are encouraged to study God as he is revealed in Scripture. The more fully we grasp his character and the ways he patiently deals with us as his children, the better prepared we will be to minister to our children in a manner pleasing to the Father.

Practicing what we preach

Earlier (Ch. 2) we noted that the Hebrew word *ben* was used of one's children. Often translated 'children of', it could refer specifically to biological offspring. However, it was also used to show that the children reflected the character of the father. In Hebrew culture, character was prized so much that it was the standard by which one's children were measured. Sadly, this is not so much the case in our day, as character is not valued in modern societies so much as success. As Christians we cannot make this trade. If we would have godly children, they need first to see God's character in us.

Godly behaviour and attitudes can be described to children, but are best viewed in living examples. As Ray Anderson notes, 'Character is what children perceive in the lives of their parents, not what the parent prescribes as the rule for the children.'[1] With the exception of the Bible itself, our lives are the most important book on biblical character our children will ever read. A central component of the family that nurtures faith is the understanding and demonstration of godly character. As I often quip to the parents I work with, 'You can be no better as a parent than you are as a person.'

Let us begin by taking a few glimpses into Scripture to see what is expected of us. First, Christian character is best summarized as a fulfilling of the Great Commandment, 'Love the Lord your God with all your heart and with all your soul and with all your mind' (Matt. 22:37). While this sounds obvious, I have seen a tendency in some Christian circles to stress the family to such an extent that 'familyolatry' almost results. Jesus makes clear in Matthew 10:37 that anyone who loves his son or daughter more than Jesus is not worthy of him. Our children need to understand that they are not the greatest love of their parents' lives, but that God is. This is a challenge to us. Most parents don't need prodding to spend time with their children or to try to talk with them. However, our walk with God is often a different matter as we struggle to make time to pray or study the Bible. I fear for many of us this betrays a love for God that is weak and in violation of the Great Commandment. It will be hard to expect our children to love God intently if they do not see such love in our lives. Conversely, Jesus notes in the same text that loving our parents more than him is also unworthy. It is a strange thing to desire that our children love someone else more than us, but this is right so long as the object of their affections is their heavenly Father.

How will they see this love? Most of all it will be natural as they hear us spontaneously speak of him through the day. They will notice that we pray, that we are grieved by the things that grieve God, and that we invest valuable time and energy into spiritual devotion.

Meanwhile, back to Matthew 22. The Great Commandment is followed by another, namely 'Love your neighbour as yourself' (v. 39). Here is another lofty challenge. Loving our neighbours is immensely difficult, and it is an area where the world has seen Christians fall short. If we interpret our neighbour as anyone whose life touches ours, then we must include in this Jesus' command to love our enemies (Matt. 5:44). Our children see us when we are angry with the slow driver in front of us, irritated by the neighbour who never brought back the serving dish she borrowed, or hostile toward those who openly live sinful lifestyles.

Jesus informs us that if we love only those who love us, we are no better than the tax-collectors or pagans (Matt. 5:46–7). Not only must we learn to love our enemies, we must then teach this love to our children.

I encourage you to spend some time in reflection, asking God to show you how you fare in love for him and for others, including your enemies. Pray that he will show you particular areas of shortcoming. Seek his grace and guidance to grow in these.

BLESSED QUALITIES

While love for God and neighbour summarizes the Law, it is helpful to speak more specifically about the character traits that should mark our lives. I would point to two lists in Scripture that serve as guides to Christian character.

The first, in keeping with our theme in the past few pages, comes from Matthew and is found in the Beatitudes. Matthew 5 describes these qualities and their accompanying blessings. I will offer only a few words on each in relating them to our lives as witnessed by our children.

Poverty of spirit contrasts with the self-esteem movement of our day. Children who see this in their parents' lives learn that there is Someone greater from whom to glean significance. Children also do well to see us mourn. Though there is a tendency to hide this from them, they benefit from learning the things that grieve our spirits. This may be the death of a loved one, but can also include sin and suffering. Meekness in our lives shows our children that we don't have to exert our energies to be seen favourably, but that we entrust our well being to the One who is all-powerful. How vital it is for our children to see us as believers who have insatiable appetites for righteousness, hungering and thirsting after it with great intensity.

Given the mercy God has shown us, it follows that we should be examples in showing mercy to others, including our children at times. In our day of superficiality of character, purity of heart conveys to our children the sincerity of our faith in Christ. While neighbours may teach their children how to fend for themselves in fights, we are called to exemplify peacemaking for our children to see. Finally, if we live this way, we will draw negative reactions and persecution. We are to teach our children that bearing up under such circumstances is cause for blessedness from a Saviour who certainly experienced it himself.

I recommend that you take time to contemplate these qualities. Martyn Lloyd-Jones' *Studies in the Sermon on the Mount* is a wonderful place to start a more in-depth look at these.

GOD'S FRUIT IN OUR OWN LIVES

The second list I commend to you is the fruit of the Spirit described in Galatians 5:22–3. Note first that these are not qualities that we can manufacture on our own, but are the result of the work of the Holy Spirit in our lives. (The same may also be said of the Beatitudes). Love is listed first, because through it we fulfil the Great Commandment presented above. Joy is a quality strangely missing in many Christian homes, often due to a loss of a heavenly perspective on life or an overemphasis on law as opposed to grace. Peace is the opposite of anxiety, and is rooted in a deep faith in God. Patience is a prayer of many parents, for children can serve as a primary test here. Kindness is a dying virtue in our times, and one our children especially need to see in our lives as it is increasingly rare. Our children are encouraged when they see goodness in our lives, a sign of genuineness of our faith.

Faithfulness stands out against a backdrop of unreliable people that our children encounter. One of the most common complaints I hear from children is that their friends are unfaithful. Here is an opportunity to make family more attractive than peers. Gentleness is an interesting trait to be included here. It is tempting for parents to stress 'assertiveness' in unhealthy ways, advising their children to stand up for themselves and their rights. Children of Christians should see in their parents' lives the gentleness that characterized the life of Jesus. Finally, in a time when 'just do it' is the mantra for giving in to your impulses and feelings, children desperately need to see a life of self-control in their parents. This is especially difficult when our children anger us. Even when we punish our children, they should see our lives as under control, guided by the Spirit who dwells within us.

These lists are merely designed to stimulate your thinking on how the godly character of parents contributes to an environment that is spiritually fertile for children. I trust you might add other qualities to these (e.g. Proverbs 31 offers a thorough description of a godly wife and mother). However, the best summary of godliness is simply that parents are to fear God, for as Proverbs 14:26 observes, 'He who fears the LORD has a secure fortress, and for his children it will be a refuge.' I pray that you join me in prayer to grow in these qualities and others taught in the Scriptures.

Ephesians and the Family

One of the central texts on the Christian home is Ephesians 5–6. One finds here guidance for godly family relationships along a number of dimensions. Yes, we will cover 'Children, obey your parents' (6:1), but will save that for a separate chapter on children's responsibilities (Ch. 8). For now, we look at Paul's admonitions for couples and fathers.

AN ATTRACTIVE MARRIAGE

Sadly, I've spoken with too many children who say they plan never to marry because of the poor relationship they have witnessed between their parents. Since marriage is a creation ordinance, and to be a model of the union of Christ and his church, the marriage of their parents should be attractive to children. They should learn from it how relationships should be and be inspired to model it in their own marriage in the future.

Ephesians 5:33 summarizes Paul's section on marriages (vv. 22–33): 'Each one of you must love his wife as he loves himself, and the wife must respect her husband.' Let's look briefly at these two commands.

Paul begins in verse 22 with wives, so we will follow his lead. Few topics in Scripture can raise blood pressure like the issue of wives being subject to husbands. None the less, this is biblical and cannot be dodged (though it is beyond the scope of this work to explain the 'whys' of it). Paul's argument is that this submission should reflect that of the church to Christ. This is important because the marriage of a child's parents affords that child a view of how a life of obedience and submission is lived out in human relations, providing an example of how he or she should submit to Christ as part of his bride, the church.

Therefore, it is crucial that wives take this calling seriously. As John Calvin notes, 'Not that the authority is equal, but wives cannot obey Christ without yielding obedience to their husbands.'[2] Herein children see obedience on two levels simultaneously, and learn.

Husbands, in contrast, are to love their wives (v. 25, 33) and in so doing provide living illustration of Christ's love for the church. The nature of this love is summarized by Matthew Henry, 'Which love of his [Christ's] is a sincere, a pure, an ardent, and a constant affection, and that notwithstanding the imperfections and failures that she [the church] is guilty of.'[3] No wife of a husband showing such love need worry about his abusing his authority, just as no child of God need worry about how he is to be cared for by Christ (see Rom. 8:38–9). Our children are blessed when they can see such love in their fathers and catch a glimpse of the greatness of God's love for them.

The intricacies of a healthy marital relationship have filled the pages of many books, and rightly so for building a strong marriage is no accident. Important as the husband–wife relationship is on its own, it provides a vital context for demonstrating biblical principles to the children born to it. Parents with a poor marriage will be ill equipped to provide a peaceful, loving home to children. Healthy relationships require ongoing effort from both spouses, a commitment to prayer for each other, and deliberate attention to the relationship through 'dates', Bible study, and jointly reading Christian books on marriage. How might you and your mate take steps to strengthen your marriage and thus provide a more powerful example to your children?

I understand there are couples where one spouse is not motivated to seek the Lord, and some families have only one parent. God can work in these situations as well. Some of the most spiritually earnest people I have met were single parents, and, while this is not the ideal, I believe God uses their faith to teach their children as well.

TRAINING WITHOUT EXASPERATING

Paul's admonition to fathers comes in Ephesians 6:4 where he writes, 'Fathers, do not exasperate your children; instead, bring them up in the training and instruction of the Lord.' Importantly, this argues that the primary parental responsibility falls on fathers. This doesn't surprise us, though we know in modern society mothers do more parenting in most families than fathers. Should that be? Even if fathers spend less time with their children than mothers do, they should take the lead in establishing household policies and practices (including the mother in the process, of course).

How important is this? The biblical requirements to be a deacon or elder state that a man must manage his family well and see that his children obey him (1 Tim. 3:4–5, 12). Titus 1:6 specifically adds that an elder's children must be believers. It is, then, important enough to deprive a man of church office if he fails in it. But when fathers fail here, there is also the inevitable fallout in their families.

As we discuss these verses, however, I wish to include mothers also. While they are not specifically listed, they certainly play roles in the matters Paul describes and should consider themselves responsible for living by Paul's words as well.

Note that the negative command precedes the positive one. The word 'exasperate' (in the NIV) is 'provoke to anger' in the New American Standard Version. Parents are not intentionally to do things to anger their children. In the parallel passage of Colossians 3:21, the NASV uses 'exasperate' while the NIV says not to 'embitter' children. Why is this important? Lest the children become discouraged. Calvin explains, 'Kind and liberal treatment has rather a tendency to cherish reverence for their parents, and to increase the cheerfulness and activity of their obedience, while a harsh and unkind manner rouses them to obstinacy and destroys the natural affections [emotions].[4] The danger is that parents become so focused on obedience that they create excessively strict rules and consequences that provoke anger and bitterness. In other cases fathers may feel their authority justifies their venting their anger. This is not to be, says the Apostle.

Children have some sense of fairness, part of the image of God that is present though distorted. They can sense unreasonableness in their parents many times, and react against it. I see this most often when teenagers are obedient and responsible, but their parents, out of fear of the world, deny privileges and opportunities. They wish to protect their children, but the teenager more often sees this as not trusting them despite their good behaviour.

Parents often appropriately punish children for sinful actions, but do so in an excessive manner. We will speak of this more in Chapter 7, but here suffice it to say that more is not always better. Parents can anger their children also by rebuking them for behaviour that is irritating but not sinful. Being in a bad mood yourself is not justification for punishing children for behaviour that is normally acceptable.

One of the most tragic things I hear children say is that they feel, no matter what they do, they cannot please their parents. While no child is perfect, we as parents are to be careful not to frustrate our children by always demanding more and never praising successes.

Search your own life, and talk with your spouse. Do you have attitudes or act in ways that exasperate your children or discourage them? This might involve the humbling task of approaching your children and asking whether they find you unfair or frustrating in any ways. When they are right, ask their forgiveness and let them know that, by God's grace, you will do better.

Now for the positive side. We are to bring our children up in the 'training and instruction of the Lord'. Observe first that the Greek for 'bring up', according to Calvin,[5] unquestionably carries the idea of gentleness and forbearance. Lovingkindness is to underlie our training and education of our children. Just teaching or disciplining them is insufficient. It must be done lovingly and gently.

Let us now consider the key words in the command: 'training' and 'instruction', which in Greek are *paidea* and *nouthesia*. The former is related to the word for 'child' and carries a fairly broad idea of child-raising. The idea may be clearer if we think of training in a sport today, say soccer. A coach may instruct you in strategy so you have a thorough working knowledge of the game. But he will do much more. He will train you physically by getting you into excellent shape and drilling you on skills such as dribbling and passing. Similarly, the notion here is that parents are to do more than just teach their children a set of facts, but to train them in all their experience to love and serve God.

Nouthesia is a more cognitive word, being related to *nous*, or mind. It carries the idea of instructing the mind. Still, it has a broader implication than just factual knowledge, seeking to impact the will and disposition as well.[6] This is why it has the more academic translation of 'instruction', and can also mean 'warning'.

It is the intent of this entire work to guide you in training your children, so I offer no particular comments here. Instruction as education is the subject of Chapter 8, so I refer you there for a discussion of training. Allow me to bring to your attention here, however, that both training and instruction are to be 'of the Lord'. The goals and the content of our training and instructing are to be God's, not ours. It is easy, for example, to see knowledge as a means to financial success for our children. Sorting out our 'hidden agendas' in parenting can be challenging, but this is needful if we are to approach this biblical standard.

Praying for—and with—our children

I doubt there has ever been a Christian parent who did not pray for his or her children, so at one level I assume you pray for your children, and/or the children under your care in ministry. So, the issue here is not whether we pray for our children, but how.

We must pray for our children frequently. Daily prayer is a minimum. Above that, we do well to offer spontaneous prayers as matters with our children come to our attention. We need to pray regularly. If you are like me, unless you designate a time and place for prayer in your schedule, it tends not to happen. Our children are vital elements of any prayer list for our designated prayer times. We also need to pray intensely. I fear focused prayer is a lost art in modern days. Our prayers are often riddled with cliches, showing little thought and following familiar paths. As we saw earlier, our children face an extremely hostile culture today, and they need prayer that is as deliberate and sincere as are the forces that compete for their souls.

We need to pray specifically for our children. 'God bless Johnny' is a great place to start, but we must go far beyond this. I suggest praying the Beatitudes and the fruit of the Spirit passages for your believing children. You might also add prayers that their minds will be filled with the thoughts of Philippians 4:8. Pray that they would be guarded from error by the Ten Commandments, noting each one separately. Children need prayer for faith: saving faith, sustaining faith, faith to live biblically. I believe you could add others topics to this list, including the day-to-day struggles our precious ones face. Prayer for our children needs to be done by each parent separately, but also together.

Children are the proper subjects of prayers of the church leadership and in public worship. Our church has a specific time set aside for people to pray for our youth, and such times are quite fruitful in guarding our little ones and cultivating their growth.

We also need to pray with our children. They need to see that we pray for them and the way we do it. This, of course, needs to be done lovingly and not as a spiritualized list of our complaints about them. This way they learn more of how to pray for themselves, and hopefully for us as well. Have them make requests and pray together for them, gradually shaping these away from the selfish desires that so often muddle our prayers to petitions that seek the glory of God.

Finally, pray for yourself as a parent. Ask for strength for the task, wisdom to make good decisions, for patience, grace, endurance, and whatever else you need. Pray for other parents and their children also, sharing their burdens. Ours is not the only garden that matters.

Family Worship

This may be a strange sounding phrase to many of us. We are more accustomed to the more modern term 'family devotions'. I fear, though, that this is more than a matter of semantics. Let me explain.

'Devotions' carries the notion of brief times of expressing your commitment to God. This, of course, is by no means bad. In contrast, 'family worship' carries the breadth of meaning that worship includes. It is coming into the presence of God as a household congregation for the purpose of offering him worship. These times should be unhurried, planned times of coming into the presence of God. There should be a richness in these times together, a quality hard to find in simply reading a one-page devotional and offering a brief prayer.

I know of no better work on the subject than J. W. Alexander's *Thoughts on Family Worship*, and I commend it to you.[7] The topic deserves a book of its own. However, let me lay out a few suggestions for you to consider.

First, a regular time and place is fundamental. As difficult as it is for individuals to find time for worship, getting an entire family together is nearly impossible unless there is a definite time. The parents must make this a priority in their own schedule and then ensure that it is reserved for their children as well. (This is especially challenging if you have teenagers.) It is best to share these times in a certain place in the house if only to have more of a 'set aside' sense to the time you share.

What of the content of the times of family worship? I suggest three main components: study, prayer, and singing.

The father as head of household should plan and lead a study of the Bible. Various plans can be used, but it is desirable that it be more than a reading of a passage. He can explain the text to the family, or, better yet, lead them into understanding through guided questions. (Be careful to avoid this disintegrating into a 'what it means to me' session as this can stray from the intended meaning of the biblical authors.) Doctrines taught in the passage can be drawn out, and specific applications made. The family worship time can also be a time to review catechisms being taught (more on this in the next chapter.)

Prayer is another part of the agenda. Some requests may flow from the application of the passage being studied. Individual members of the family may make requests. Other loved ones should be remembered as well as the church, its leaders and missionaries. Specific individuals that family members are trying to reach out to (such as children at school or co-workers at the office) can be mentioned as well. The format can vary, but it is good to have each family member participate.

Finally, singing is important. My family has enjoyed a practice of learning a hymn each week, taking time to discuss the meaning of each verse as we learn it. This is also helpful in preparing children to participate in public worship. If someone can play an instrument, that's great. But even *a cappella* the sounds of a family singing together are pleasing in the sight of God. Notice that I mentioned hymns. The great hymns are generally rich in their focus on God and on truths about him. Contemporary Christian music very often seems obsessed with the individual to the neglect of God. I do not oppose more recent music, but be sure to edit what you include for doctrinal soundness and Godward focus.

The structure and order of these components may vary. You may also include traditional items such as recital of the Lord's Prayer or the Apostles' Creed. Singing the Doxology or *Gloria Patri* can also be meaningful traditions to include. The worship itself should bring glory to God, but the process also teaches our children how important our faith is, while the tradition itself can draw the family together. (Other traditions, such as holiday activities, vacations, or 'family game night' enrich the soil of the family and are not to be neglected.)

I know for many of those who read this the idea of family worship sounds good, but you doubt you can get one or more of your children to participate. This is less of a problem with younger children, but can be quite an issue with teenagers. I suggest you bear in mind what we said earlier about not exasperating them. You may require them to join you but not require them to participate, or you may leave them the option of joining you in cases where resistance is great. They will still see your example, and, while you may force them to be with you, you cannot force true worship.

Alexander recommends worship times in the mornings and evenings. Frankly I have not succeeded in getting my crew together for much time in the mornings. For many families, that may be a proper time for 'devotions'. Of course, aim for consistency in your times, but avoid legalism and realize that occasionally your plans will be thwarted.

WORSHIPPING WITH THE FAMILY OF GOD

As important as family worship is to the nurturance of our spiritual seedlings, coming before God together with other families and individuals in the body of Christ is vital and not to be forsaken (Heb. 10:25). We will discuss the place of children in corporate worship in Chapter 11, but a few items merit inclusion here.

To begin, I want to stress the importance of commitment to a local congregation. Many believers today enjoy the private aspects of the faith and shun involvement in a local church beyond sitting in the worship services. This is often justified by complaints about the formal church, or denying the need for such, or simply the preference to seek God independently.

Here again we fall prey to individualistic secular thought as we overlook the importance of being under the spiritual authority of the church. As parents, this can communicate to our children that we see ourselves as adequate authorities. If they take that attitude toward us, we probably won't be appreciative. Moreover, the positive aspects of commitment to a local church include fellowship, prayer support, educational programmes, and shepherding. I commend to you the exceeding value of whole-hearted participation in your local congregation.

The worship service at your church should be directed toward God and not have as a goal entertainment of the audience. While beautiful music and interesting sermons can steer our hearts toward heaven, they can also shift our gaze onto our own pleasures and away from God. If we do not want our children to be self-serving, we need to teach them the Other-directedness of worship.

There is wisdom in the idea that the Sabbath began at sundown the night before. This affords a time to quiet our souls, collect our thoughts, and prepare our hearts for meeting God the next day. It is regrettable that today Saturday nights are busy for most families, often with activities that keep them up late. Not only does this deny them opportunity to prepare for Sunday worship, but also promotes sleeping till the last minute, hurrying to get ready, and challenging the speed limit on the way to church. Often this frenzy leaves family members irritated with one another and in a poor mood to worship once they get there.

Ideally, Saturday night's family worship can set the stage for joining the larger body the next day. A good night's sleep leads to an earlier awakening and time to prepare ourselves spiritually for the services to come.

The worship services themselves can serve as teaching opportunities for parents as they instruct their children in the liturgy and its meaning. Once they are on their way home, fathers can lead in a discussion of what was learned in the worship time and in Sunday school. It is frighteningly easy to come away from church talking about the latest social news, even to the point of gossip. As parents who want to cultivate godliness in our children, we must avoid such error and fully utilize time at church toward our parenting goals.

In these pages we have seen the goal of parenting and ways that Christian parents can direct their efforts toward it, providing a context that is rich in the nutrients needed for the spiritual growth of our children. May our Heavenly Father grant us grace to see where we need to improve and give us initiative to make the changes needed.

THE SCHOOL OF LIFE:
PARENTS ARE TEACHERS

'Education without [Christian] values, as useful as it is, seems rather to make man a more clever devil' (C. S. Lewis).

'We shall never learn to feel and respect our real calling and destiny, unless we have taught ourselves to consider everything as moonshine, compared with the education of the heart' (Sir Walter Scott).

Sally loves her school. The teacher does little except when one child hurts another. There are no lessons planned and no assignments. While there are a few books in the classroom, the kids ignore them as they focus on the toys. No tests. No homework. Just playing all day long without interruption. No wonder Sally loves her school.

Obviously there's a problem here. No parent I know of would send their child to Sally's school. When we send a child to school, we assume that they will learn there. We trust they are in the hands of a teacher who has a plan for what they are to learn and what lessons are needed to teach it to them. We expect the teacher to have the day organized and to keep the students on track. We anticipate our child learning to read, write, do maths, and have some understanding of the world around him or her.

These goals cannot be accomplished if the teacher doesn't know his or her role and guide the children into theirs.

We are about to learn how clearly the Bible places parents in the role of spiritual teachers. While we generally want our children to be biblically literate and spiritually sensitive, we frequently lack a 'curriculum' by which we intend to reach this goal. Just as we would not want our children in Sally's school, we should aspire to provide a context for Christian education for our children that is planned and deliberate. Let's examine God's Word on the subject.

Parents are teachers

The first reference to a parent as a teacher goes all the way back to Abraham. In Genesis 18:19, God speaks as he prepares to destroy Sodom and Gomorrah: 'I have chosen him [Abraham], so that he will direct his children and his household after him to keep the way of the Lord by doing what is right and just, so that the Lord will bring about for Abraham what he has promised him.'

God's promise, of course, was to make of Abraham a great nation (e.g. Gen. 12:2). Our text seems to imply that part of the way God intended to bring about his promise was for Abraham's descendents to continue in 'the way of the Lord by doing what is right and just'. How were they to know what was the way of the Lord? Abraham was to direct them, or 'command' as the New American Standard Version renders it. It was Abraham's task to teach his descendents God's ways and command them to keep them. Here is our first glimpse of God's strategy of propagating people of faith through parental instruction and guidance.

God's intentions are more explicit when we reach Moses. As God communicates his law to the people through Moses, his servant declares:

> These commandments that I give you today are to be upon your hearts. Impress them on your children. Talk about them when you sit at home and when you walk along the road, when you lie down and when you get up. Tie them as symbols on your hands and bind them on your foreheads. Write them on the door-frames of your houses and on your gates (Deut. 6:6–9).

This command follows the 'second printing' of the Ten Commandments and their summary as what Jesus later called the Great Commandment to love God. These commandments were not just for a one-time hearing for the immediate audience. They were to be rehearsed and passed on to subsequent generations.

Notice that these verses give almost a 'lesson plan'. First, the goal was not mere memorization, but to impress God's law on the heart. By this is meant an absorption into one's personality and life, not just a passing on of 'data'. This is why the rehearsal and application that follow are so crucial.

God's law was to be 'impressed' on children, talked about in all situations, tied as symbols and written in conspicuous places. We will not go into each of these, but merely stress that these 'lessons' were to be given in a variety of manners and places. The responsibility for this rested primarily on the parents. There is even an expectation that the teaching of the law will provide parents with occasion to share history lessons with their children (Deut. 6:20–25).

It is undeniable that God intended parents to be teachers of the ways of righteousness, and that this was to be quite systematic and frequent. In contrast, parents today are tempted to feel satisfied that their children are learning the Bible in Sunday school, or at a Christian school. But this falls far short of the biblical mandate for parents to teach God's ways themselves and in various contexts. We are God's primary instructors, and too easily slip into the ways of Sally's teacher.

If we are teachers, what is our curriculum? Scripture holds our answer.

The content of our teaching

Deuteronomy 6 gives us a jump-start on our curriculum. We are to teach our children God's law. Many Christians today argue that this is no longer important, but that is not true. Granted, we are free from the law as a way of salvation since Christ fulfilled it for us. But our children need to learn God's standards as 'schoolmaster' (Gal. 3:24–5, KJV) to show them their sin and point them to their need of a Saviour. One of the great omissions in Christian teaching today is the seriousness and pervasiveness of sin. Teaching God's law will help our children appreciate their fallenness and need for a Saviour.

Once our children profess Christ, the law still serves as a 'roadmap' for righteous living. Though we no longer need to keep it in order to be righteous, it still reflects God's moral character and we (and our children) are to imitate that. As we saw in our discussion of godly parents, the Great Commandment was reiterated by Jesus and is certainly relevant today.

Proverbs 1:7 proclaims, 'The fear of the LORD is the beginning of knowledge.' The pivotal point of a Christian education is to teach children the fear of the Lord. This is a formidable term to define, though the traditional summary of 'reverential awe' serves fairly well. Jerry Bridges, in his commendable book on the subject, explains that 'a profound sense of awe toward God is undoubtedly the dominant element in the attitude or set of emotions that the Bible calls "the fear of God".'[1]

This is strategic territory, because one of the great problems of modern Christians is the 'shrinking of God' as we have shunned studying his character and greatness and focused on how he can be useful to us. As a result, there is a 'weightlessness' to God[2] in the church, where we praise him and speak of him, but have little grasp of his awesomeness and power. Parents who teach their children about the character and attributes of God can help their children understand how truly great God is. Then it is natural to fear him in the biblical sense. At this point wisdom has taken root.

Proverbs has much more to offer than one verse, as most of it is written as advice of a father to his son. It is quite reasonable then to see this book as a vital part of the Christian parent's curriculum. Systematic reading and teaching from Proverbs will greatly contribute to training children in the ways of God. Parents can take these truths and help their children think through applications for today.

By the time we reach the New Testament, Paul makes explicit the fact that 'all Scripture…is useful for teaching, rebuking, correcting and training in righteousness' (2 Tim. 3:16). We are to strive to teach our children the 'full counsel of God' contained in the Scriptures. Recall from Deuteronomy 6 that this is not trivia we are teaching, but truth that is to be inscribed on the hearts of our children. Such learning will not occur by accident, but will require of us time and energy, and something of a plan.

The context of our teaching

Scripture teaches us plainly that the core of the parent's curriculum is the Bible itself. How is it to be taught? Moses instructed the Hebrews to teach it throughout the day in a variety of contexts. Let's see what these might be today.

We discussed family worship in the previous chapter, and this can serve the purpose of education as well as worship. In selecting topics for reading and study, consider the areas where your family needs instruction the most.

Catechizing is almost a lost art, but it still survives in some corners of many traditions. Early in the history of the church, as it was growing into heathen territory, converts were instructed in the doctrines of the church before being formally admitted to membership. This formalized style of instruction also came to be practised with the children of believers, providing a systematic way of training them in the truths of the faith. In Puritan times this was seen as being so important that churches were encouraged to purchase the catechisms for each family, with the pastor hand-delivering them to each household and following up to see how the process was going.[3]

Most denominations have a catechism available. One of the most widely used is *The Westminster Shorter Catechism* (or, of course, for the heartier types, *The Larger Catechism*). A Children's Catechism has been adapted from this to make the great truths of the faith accessible to children as early as the preschool years.

Catechisms are intended to be learned systematically and memorized. Regular times should be set aside for teaching your children a catechism, and they should be encouraged to practise between lessons. Yet, your goal is not reached if they merely memorize; recall that the truths are to be inscribed on their hearts. This will require helping them to think through the significance of what they are learning in practical settings. (Preparing to teach our children in this way will have the 'side effect' of enhancing our grasp of these great truths as well.)

Moses made clear that his hearers were to discuss the Law frequently. Our teaching of the Word should occur in the midst of our day-to-day activities. We naturally bring to mind things that interest us. As well as I know that my wife shares little of my enthusiasm for basketball, I still spontaneously comment to her about the latest development. (And she patiently listens!) It should be just as natural for us to bring up the things of God in our general conversation, assuming we love him more than other things in our lives. It is easy to compartmentalize our lives, discussing spiritual things at 'spiritual times', such as family worship, while getting caught up in the affairs of daily life the rest of the day. Moses exhorts us to avoid such separation. We are to look for God's hands in all the events of the day and to deal with them in terms of God's actions. In doing so, not only are we more mindful of the sovereign God, but our children learn how to perceive God in all of life.

There is deliberateness to the teaching described in Deuteronomy 6, and this suggests we are to find opportunities to teach spiritual truths. I encourage you to plan homework assignments and field trips to reinforce what you teach your children. If you are teaching gratitude, have your children write 'thank you notes' to those who have done things for them. If you are covering compassion, have them help serve a meal at a homeless shelter. If you are stressing gentleness, take your children to a nursing home and have them interview a resident. I think you get the idea, and can see that there are limitless possibilities here.

Finally, in no way do I want to minimize the importance of the teaching that goes on in Sunday schools, Christian schools, and various youth groups. I only hope to shift your thinking to seeing these as supplemental sources for your children's training. These activities provide the 'amen' that shows your children the agreement within the body of Christ.

Related areas of instruction

I offer a few suggestions for related areas where parents are instrumental in shaping the thinking of their children, and suggest some practical ways of enriching your children's understanding of the application of biblical principles.

Psychologists have rigorously studied the moral thinking of children and found that they grow in how they go about making decisions about what is right and wrong. Sadly, most of this research is disinterested in *what* the children consider right and wrong, choosing to focus on *how* they go about making their decisions.

Christians are definitely concerned with right and wrong and labour to help their children understand these concepts biblically. However, we may be more successful if we work actively with our little ones to see how they are making their moral decisions. We can then guide them into more appropriate ways of thinking.

This is difficult to summarize in a few sentences, so a couple of examples may help you understand what I am saying. When a young child refuses to share, you are right in pointing out that selfishness is wrong. However, you may learn that your child is choosing to keep his or her toys because he or she lacks any idea of how his or her actions impact the other child involved. Help your child think through how the other child might feel and what benefits may come from sharing. This way you can enhance your child's sense of empathy.

Of course this sounds a bit like teaching the Golden Rule spoken by Jesus in Matthew 7:12: '...do to others what you would have them do to you'. Fulfilling this requires the child to develop what psychologists call 'perspective taking', the ability to view a situation from the perspective of another person. Rehearsing this skill with our children can help them become more sensitive to the feelings of others and develop a better grasp of how to live out the Golden Rule.

The nature of formal education has changed dramatically. A staple of traditional education was logic. Since rationality is part of the image of God, consistent and accurate use of it is important. If your children are in a school that offers a course in logic, have them take it. If not, get a book on the subject and teach it yourself. Accurate reasoning and problem solving are vital skills in all areas of life, but are particularly useful in challenging the philosophies of the world from a Christian perspective.

In addition to formal instruction, parents can encourage their children to be active thinkers. This is a formidable task in a day where the media trains our children to be passive thinkers. One of the attractions of television and movies is that they require no thinking: one sits back and soaks. This is dangerous because it is poor training for young minds, but also because there is so much irrational material in the media.

As a counsellor, I have often wished I could accomplish in a half dozen counselling sessions the change that happens to families in thirty minutes (and even less if you exclude time for commercials) on television. This is possible because the twists of these plots are unrealistic. Yet, if you watch these unthinkingly, you may think that is how problems ought to be resolved: quickly and without clear reason.

While I admit it is doubtful that we can keep our children from being exposed to the media, we can use it to our advantage. Watch television with your children, and take advantage of the lengthy commercial breaks to discuss the logic and sense of the plot. Teach your children to pay attention to the flow of the dialogue and see if it is logical. Have them consider the emotional responses of people and see if they are justified. Ask them if they think the solutions to problems on the programmes will work in real life. Suddenly, watching television is no longer passive and may even lead to your children becoming critical thinkers.

FINANCIAL WISDOM

One last area I want to mention is training your children in financial stewardship. Proverbs contains much advice about the financial benefits of labour, and the Bible in general is not shy about the subject. I would venture a few suggestions for parents.

Most children these days feel overworked if asked to make up their beds. Yet, children throughout history have been expected to share in the work of the family. (Recall from Chapter 2 that this is one reason why they were valued.) Parents therefore should expect their children to share in household chores, with the number of these increasing with the age of the child. Some should be simply contributions to the family. Some of the chores, I believe, should be compensated with an allowance.

Why? Primarily I suggest this because it affords an opportunity to learn stewardship, especially for children too young to do work outside the home. From the allowance, children can learn giving to the work of God, saving, and making financial decisions. Allowances often fail because the parents give the child additional money for purchases, rendering the allowance money useless and lowering motivation to do the work to earn the money. (I admit I would work less too if someone else covered all my financial needs.)

So, it is important to establish with the allowance an area of purchases that must come out of the allowance. For younger children, this will likely be snacks or toys. As the child grows, so should the number of chores, the allowance, and the area of financial responsibility. By their early teens children should be expected to cover all of their entertainment expenses, some of their transportation costs, and some costs for special events such as school trips. Later in adolescence, young people should also be responsible for a clothing budget, a share of automobile expenses, and costs associated with social activities. The parents must be wise in making the amount of allowance fit the amount of responsibility, but if this is done well, the child learns to manage money as he or she matures. This way he or she is better prepared for life away from the 'nest', be it college or a first apartment.

ACADEMIC CHOICES

We have covered some indispensable areas of Christian training, but have yet to examine the most common area: formal academic education. Formal education is a Christian value for, as we saw in Chapter 3, it is a type of rebuilding the image of God. Yet, this is an area that is hotly debated both within and outside the church. Public education has drawn criticism from all sides, yet probably the majority of children of Christians get their education by this means. Private Christian schools have sprouted around the world, offering Christian parents an option to troubled public schools, but with a price. Home-schooling has become the choice for rapidly increasing numbers, but this approach is not without its critics. Which is right for your child? A formal education is essential to fulfilling our call as parents, and few choices play as large a role in shaping the lives of our children as where to educate them.

I will not tell you the answer, except the popular one, 'It depends.' I offer a brief survey of some of the points in favour of and against the three options mentioned, and then submit a series of variables to consider in your equation for choosing a schooling option.

PUBLIC SCHOOLS

Throughout history parents have been the primary teachers of children in most cases, though others took responsibility from the parents from early times (see, for example, Gal. 4:2). As education has become more technical, driven by a better understanding of how children learn, it became advisable to have children taught by those better trained than parents. In addition, the explosion of knowledge has made it difficult for parents to know enough to teach their children more technical subjects. There is thus a case for others educating our children.

Public schools as we know them came into being only early in the twentieth century, offering opportunity for all children to have a chance at a formal education. Such training previously had been the privilege of those with greater financial resources. (Though interestingly in early America the pastor of the village church was generally responsible for seeing that the children were educated.) Now opportunity is there for any child to be educated. In fact there is more than opportunity, there is a legal requirement.

Public schools offer Christian children a taste of the 'real world', exposing them to children of a variety of backgrounds and beliefs. If education is defined more broadly, such exposure is an important part of it. This affords Christian children early occasion to learn what it is to be salt and light in the modern world. By withdrawing from public schools, we remove their salt and speed their decay. If children will have to live their faith in the real world, then public schools can better prepare them. Finally, public schools offer the widest array of resources, especially for those children with special needs.

Public schools have their down side, of course. In America in particular, safety has become a major issue as children increasingly carry weapons to school and show a tendency toward aggression. Many have also raised questions about the quality of public education as schools deal with unmotivated students and discouraged teachers.

But Christian parents have another set of issues with public schools. The banishment of Christian thought from the classroom leads students to think that the world is understandable apart from God, religion simply being a 'corner' of the world excluded from the discussion. Such an approach is, in the truest sense of the word, 'a-theistic', or 'no-god'. Christian children should learn that God rules all things in his providence and no field of study is to be separated from his influence. This is hard to do in public schools, especially for the younger children.

Finally, while the idea of being salt and light is important, one can question whether five and six year olds grasp this well enough to stand against the influences they encounter. God is indeed almighty, but we must be careful not to test him unnecessarily. Young children are vulnerable to the subtle educational philosophies and the powerful influences of peers who prematurely expose them to language, sexual concepts, and other areas that push the limits of their ability to withstand temptation.

CHRISTIAN SCHOOLS

The founding of Christian schools has been a tradition of the faith for some time, claiming the great reformer Martin Luther as one of its advocates nearly 500 years ago. Such schools vary in their orientation, some simply offering Bible and chapel while others integrate faith into all areas of the curriculum. These schools still offer well-trained teachers and exposure to areas such as music, art and athletics. Such schools offer children a peer group that shares their faith, though obviously Christian children stray at times, and no school is immune from behaviour problems.

Christian schools, however, are generally quite expensive which limits access to those who are more financially secure. While the teachers are generally well-trained, they still must deal mostly with groups of children, meaning little attention can be paid to the curriculum needs for individual children. Many Christian schools offer some special education programmes, but generally cannot match the resources of public schools in this regard. Finally, as noted, it is almost impossible to avoid having some children who are 'trouble makers'. Our fallen nature makes erring children somehow attractive, so peers can have a negative influence on some children even in Christian schools.

HOME SCHOOL

Dramatically increasing numbers of parents (including many non-believers) are turning to home-schooling. For many it is frustration with the public schools, but for others it is the rediscovery of the joy of making family the central focus of all aspects of their lives. Home-schoolers can choose from a variety of curricula, and work at the individual child's pace in each subject. This avoids the frustration many children feel in classrooms that move too fast or too slow. Money is rarely an issue, though some materials must be purchased.

Home-school allows parents to teach children the Bible in accordance with their faith tradition and to guarantee that all subjects are taught in the light of Scripture. It also provides a better stewardship of time, as children do not usually have to wait until others are finished with a task to do something else. This also gives flexibility in scheduling so families can do more things together.

There are problems here as well. Not all parents have working relationships with their children that are adequate to teach them, leading to all-day battles over the work with little learning taking place. Individual parents cannot match a school faculty with varied strengths, creating the risk of a poorer quality education. Art, music and sports are easily overlooked, and many parents lack the training to work with special needs children.

But, the most common complaint about home-schooling is the lack of social contacts. While I know of cases where families are overly isolated, most home-schoolers join associations that provide opportunities for interaction with other students in classes, on field trips, and plain old get-togethers.

Weighing your options

As I commented previously, there is not 'the' right answer about formal education for your children. To assist you in your choices, I offer a few suggestions to ponder as you prayerfully decide.

Consider the issues. I have given some of the basic arguments, and some of these are more important to some parents than others. The weight you give to the issues listed gives guidance as to what you should do.

Consider the options in your area. Some areas have better public schools than others. Many areas have no Christian schools, or none whose approaches fit your views on education, or maybe none you can afford. Know your options before you decide.

Consider your child's needs. Some children need the individualized attention that home-schooling offers. Others need the special services of the public schools. Others need the more positive environment of a Christian school. Just as you can't buy your child clothes if you don't know his or her size, you can't choose a schooling option if you don't know his or her personality and needs.

Consider your abilities. This relates primarily to home-schooling, and points to the fact that not all parents are good candidates for teaching at home. Some have health problems, some have to work to make ends meet, and some lack the skills or rapport with their children to pull this off successfully. Also consider whether you have the necessary support from others to take on such a task, and whether there are those you can turn to for guidance when you are unsure.

Above all, talk this through with your spouse, seek godly counsel and pray. Your decision will not determine your child's life, but it certainly will influence it.

We now see that it is essential for Christian parents to see themselves as trainers in righteousness, and as the primary directors of academic education as well. I ask you now to consider what would be a good first step to take toward becoming a godlier educator for your children.

teaching her to ju
practising tossin
the disc is na
instinct.) M
right dir
dog of
T
S

/

DISCIPLINING DISCIPLES

'Even a child is known by his actions, by whether his conduct is pure and right' (Proverbs 20:11).

The greatest firmness is the greatest mercy (Henry Wadsworth Longfellow).

Snickers thinks everything in the world is a chewy toy: sticks, leaves, boards, bones, chairs, pillows, arms, legs, and even my daughter's swing set. In an effort to avoid taking out a second mortgage to buy new patio furniture (among other things), we have embarked on a fairly structured plan for tempering our young pup's zest for chewing. Certainly we don't enjoy spanking our delightful Labrador, but she needs to learn what she can chew and what she can't.

But I have another goal for Snickers. I have long wanted a 'frisbee dog', one who would gracefully track down the gliding disc, leap into the air, and make a perfect catch. I have noticed that Snickers, being the equal opportunity beast that she is, chews on a frisbee as readily as on anything else. But I haven't peeked into the back yard and found her practising her catches. I realize that if Snickers is to become the dog I want her to be, spanking her for chewing will not be enough. I have already begun systematically

...p to get the frisbee from my hand while also
... it for her to track down. (Apparently going after
...tural enough, but bringing it back is far from an
...y hope is that as I teach her, praise her steps in the
...ction and earn her trust, she will become the frisbee
... my dreams.

...aining a dog requires specific goals and organized effort.
...panking helps with some things, but is far from a comprehensive
way to shape a pet's behaviour. This may seem obvious, but in
my experience Christian parents sometimes think that is how it
is with children: spank them when they get out of bounds and
then assume they will be okay without any other help. When
children are not behaving as you wish or when they irritate you,
a good spanking is all that's needed. Many parents consult me as
a psychologist when this strategy fails. They expect me to have
some kind of deluxe punishment that, once put into practice,
will straighten up their children. But, as with Snickers, deliberate
training for positive behaviour is also needed, with punishment
following only when the child's behaviour goes beyond certain
limits.

Let me illustrate with a different picture. At about three years
of age, our daughter Erin had her first exposure to the wonderful
world of miniature golf. What a thrill she had as she bumped
the ball around with her little plastic putter. I gained a new
appreciation for the guard rails that marked the boundaries
of the playing surface. These saved me from many trips into
the surrounding landscape. But after a few shots, we realized
something was wrong. Erin was having a great time, but didn't
really grasp the goal of the game. The rails steered her back onto
the playing surface, but did not help her understand what we
wanted her to do. We then made a point of showing her the hole
and teaching her to aim for it.

In parenting, punishment is like the rails: it tells children when
they are out of bounds and points them back into acceptable
territory. However, it does not necessarily tell them what the 'goal'
of behaviour is. When you think about it, a really good putter
wouldn't even need the rails on a straight hole. If your aim is
accurate enough, boundaries are irrelevant. To make a biblical
comparison, the Ten Commandments can be seen as the rails on

our golf game with Jesus' great command to love God and your neighbour being the 'hole'. If you successfully target love, then you automatically stay in bounds of the commands. For example, you won't steal from someone you love as yourself.

We have learned in earlier chapters that godliness is the goal of parenting and parallels the 'hole' in our golf example and the successful catch for Snickers. Godly behaviour springs from godly character, and if our children simply 'stay in bounds' by not getting into trouble, we have by no means achieved our goal. This means that punishment is only one servant of the goal of godliness and not *the* tool of discipline. Yet it is a necessary servant and is most effective when in the company of guidance, teaching and rewards. Both positive and negative responses to children's behaviour offer immediate physical reminders of the spiritual consequences of their actions and are therefore integral parts of biblical parenting. If so, what does the Bible teach us about using consequences and how are we to use these principles?

Setting the stage

Let's briefly review things we covered earlier that form the foundation for using rewards and punishments for children's behaviour.

First, we saw in Chapter 3 that children have a moral impulse because they are made in God's image, but that image is distorted by sin and may not motivate them toward the goal of holiness. This is made worse by the reality of original sin that teaches us that the hearts of our little ones are by nature inclined toward evil. It is as if our 'golf balls' are weighted and tend to wobble away from the hole. It should then come as no surprise to us as parents that our children get out of bounds with their behaviour and need correction. We should anticipate this, and thus calm our tempers that sometimes flare because we don't expect our children to act badly.

This means that discipline serves to control the sinful inclinations in the hearts of children. As Proverbs 22:15 instructs, 'Folly [not goodness!] is bound up in the heart of a child, but the rod of discipline will drive it far from him.' Matthew Henry comments that folly is not just found in the heart but is bound there.[1] Those who do not believe children require discipline have somehow missed the clear teaching of Scripture that children are naturally inclined toward wrong behaviour. To deprive children of discipline is to give full reign to their sinful natures. (This may explain the success of violent children's media such as television and video games. These feed the folly bound in their hearts, which explains the natural interest children take in these destructive diversions.)

In our study, we have also realized (Ch. 5) that parenting is above all a deliberate effort to train our children into godliness. We teach them that they need a Saviour, that there are biblical standards for belief and behaviour, and that we live in a world where these go contrary to popular opinion. We organize our lives so this instruction is planned and also a part of the normal occurrences of daily life. But we understand that, despite these efforts, children will do wrong. Discipline (in the narrow sense of consequences for behaviour) is required to support our overall efforts to raise godly children, and does not stand alone.

A review of what the Bible tells us about correction and discipline will prepare us for some specific suggestions on how to use these.

Correction

When people enquire about my keyboarding skills, I often tell them that I type about thirty minutes a word. I recall my college days when my constant companion was the aromatic white liquid known as correction fluid. We were very good friends, for my fingers very often did not spell correctly the words sent down by my brain. The beauty of this substance was that it would cover my mistakes and allow me to put the right letters where they belonged. After all, that is what correction is all about.

Scripture teaches that correction, particularly with words, is one of the responsibilities of parents. Proverbs is the main location for these texts, and they include 9:8, 13:1, 15:31, 17:10, 19:25, 25:12, and 29:17. The notion is that when a child makes the incorrect response, the parent points it out, 'covers' it in the sense of having the child undo the wrong when possible, and then prompts the child to substitute the proper action. For example, a child is told to clean his room and he proceeds to toss all of his toys into the cupboard, leaving the floor clean. Correction here would mean his parents would explain the error of his ways, have him pull the toys back out of the cupboard, and place them neatly in their proper places. Punishment (in addition to correction) might be needed if the parents were confident this child knew that piling the toys in the cupboard was wrong. Either way, the goal of the whole scene is to correct the child's behaviour so that he knows what is right to do and has actually done it. Correction is more a part of the teaching than the disciplining process, but the line between the two is thin.

Another aspect of correction is pointing out the wrong behaviour of others to your child. This is valuable to do when watching television or videos. It is quite easy to find examples of people who respond incorrectly to situations. Commercial breaks are great opportunities to discuss with your children what the characters did wrong and what the proper response would have been. (It also provides the added advantage of distracting your children from the commercials that aren't good for them anyway.) The same approach can also be applied when your children see other children (or adults) fall short in their behaviour, though take care to do this tactfully. Looking at it this way, life is almost a constant teaching opportunity.

What does the Bible teach about discipline?

Spanking has received bad press over the past few years. All too often the evening news relates yet another horror story of parents cruelly beating their children. As Christians we share in the disgust of hearing that parents have used their children to vent their own frustrations, if not worse. But the societal response has been rather extreme, and many parents live in fear that the state social services will come knocking if they spank their children. The word is out among the kids, too. Many children in trouble readily threaten to call social services if their parents spank them. Christians are criticized for their commitment to spanking by a society that believes children do not need such discipline. This is largely rooted in humanist thought that values the comfort of children above their discipline.

We cannot deny that spanking is a controversial issue. As Christians we must have a solid understanding of what the Bible says about the topic before adopting a policy about punishment, for surely the stakes are high.

SCRIPTURE ON DISCIPLINE

We have already seen that biblical discipline is a total training programme with positive goals and not just a matter of punishing misdeeds. But our common use of the term discipline is more likely to refer only to spankings or other punishments. The Bible does not make this distinction, and it is vital that we see that rewards and punishments are merely a subset of the far-reaching biblical concept of discipline.

Scripture clearly asserts that discipline (broadly defined, but certainly including punishment) is essential. Proverbs in particular makes this case. Discipline shows love for the child (3:12; 13:24) and gives the child hope for the future (19:18). It benefits the parents as well by giving peace and delight (29:17). A lack of discipline can result in poverty and shame (13:18), being a negative influence on others (10:17), and even death (5:23; 15:10; 19:18; 23:14). This is an important contrast as Proverbs also says that if we use the rod the child will not die (23:13–14), suggesting that, in the long run, it may be more abusive to withhold discipline (which includes corporal punishment) than to avoid it. The sad harvest we are reaping in our current generation of children bears this out as more children die from murder, alcohol and drug abuse and suicide than from child abuse. A child without discipline is also a disgrace to her mother (29:15). Therefore, discipline is not to be withheld from a child (23:13). Parents who do not discipline their children are thus disobedient to the direction of Scripture.

In contrast, much is gained by discipline. If death comes from its lack, then life is the result of discipline well-administered (10:17). Honour (13:18), prudence (15:5), knowledge (15:32), and wisdom (29:15) are other benefits of good discipline by parents. So, Proverbs teaches that the parent who spares the rod hates his son (13:24).

Why is such discipline needed? We have seen the relation of children's bent to wrongdoing to original sin. The language Proverbs uses for this bent is 'folly', as we noted earlier from

Psalm 22:15. Original sin yields folly that must be brought under control by discipline. (But also remember that the ultimate 'cure' for sin is for it to be washed in the blood of Christ in salvation.) Apparently those who do not control folly go on to become fools who, even as adults, need the rod (Prov. 10:13; 14:3; 19:29; 26:3).

We determine, then, that the Bible places a high value on discipline in general, and that 'the rod' is part of this. What exactly does this mean?

SCRIPTURE ON THE ROD

If you have examined the references we have already covered in Proverbs, you will probably have noticed that 'discipline' and 'the rod' are used almost interchangeably to talk of parents' training their children (e.g., 23:13). Many people, however, think that any mention of the rod equals spanking as we know it today. I want to argue that this is not the case, and I will attempt to show you why from the Bible itself.

The word 'rod' is used in a variety of ways in the Old Testament, and several of them are quite literal. A rod was used to beat grain (Isa. 28:27), as a weapon (2 Sam. 23:21), and by shepherds to muster, count and protect sheep (Lev. 27:32; Ezek. 20:27; Ps. 23:4; Mic. 7:14). Of course, believers have long taken comfort in the Psalm 23 reference, but here the rod stands for God's protection and supervision of his children and is by no means to be taken only in a literal sense.

Some references do show the rod as a means of physical punishment. Exodus 21:20–21 gives laws regarding beating slaves. It was unlawful to kill a slave by beating with the rod, but no consequences followed a beating severe enough to make the slave unable to walk for a couple of days. Proverbs, as we noted, speaks of the rod being used on fools. There appears to be a very literal aspect of this, for example, in 10:13 where Solomon states: 'a rod is for the back of him who lacks judgment.' The rod is also applied to children in verses such as 13:24, 22:15 and 23:13–14. It is safe to conclude that the rod in Scripture can refer to physical punishment, even of one's own children. We also see from these texts that a beating with the rod is not the same thing as a spanking that might be done with hand or wooden spoon or paddle. The biblical use strongly suggests some type of stick or club. So, advocating spanking as we know it based on these texts can only be done by inferring that the rod compares to today's wooden spoon or paddle.

Those who say the rod and spanking are identical face several challenges. First, they are not being as literal as they may think given that they usually don't suggest the use of a baseball bat or the like. Supporters of spanking typically don't recommend literally using a rod, but suggest a wooden spoon, belt, or the like. Second, they usually discourage beating the child on the back (as described in some of our references), or as severely as slaves could be treated in the Old Testament. We must remember the laws of ancient Israel included provision for stoning a son who resisted discipline and acted quite badly (Deut. 21:18–21). Hopefully we are not ready to go that far as most biblical scholars agree that we should not follow these practices today. Finally, if they take the rod only literally, they must say that spanking is the only way to discipline children, and that doesn't hold up when we study the other uses of the term in the Bible.

There is no doubt that 'the rod' is used metaphorically, or symbolically, of a broad range of strategies for disciplining. Isaiah 10:15–17 uses the rod as a symbol of God disciplining Israel. The text speaks of disease and fire as examples of God's action, but it does not describe God literally taking a big stick and beating Israel. God speaks to Nathan regarding King David in 2 Samuel 7, and states in verse 14 that he will 'punish him with the rod of men'. God certainly caused difficult times to befall his chosen leader, but these were not literal beatings with a rod. Job refers to his afflictions (9:34) as 'God's rod' but this again was merely symbolic of a number of afflictions. Psalm 89:32 and Lamentations 3:1 offer similar instances.

We conclude from our review of Scripture that, while the rod definitely can include literally hitting a child with an object, its fullest meaning includes any form of unpleasant discipline designed to teach a lesson. This supports the use of spanking as a type of 'the rod', but we cannot go so far as to say that biblical discipline is only to include spankings. Other types of displeasing consequences also fit the idea of the 'rod'. But that's not all, folks. The Bible offers a case for the use of rewards with children, too.

THE BIBLE ON REWARDS

It is not unusual to have a parent dodge using rewards with their children because they see this as a form of bribery. If we are to look at it that way, then punishment is the equivalent of blackmail: do what I say or something bad will happen to you. The truth is that both are forms of coercion designed to alter behaviour and you can't rule out either simply because they can have negative connotations.

The Bible is not reluctant to speak of 'rewards' for those who obey God. (We must be careful here not to imply that we earn God's favour. I am merely showing that he has chosen to bless those who are faithful to him.) Looking no further than the Ten Commandments we see that God offers a special promise to those who honour their parents (Exod. 20:12), a point emphasized by Paul in Ephesians 6:3. It would seem strange for God to bless children who honour their parents but teach the parents that blessing those same children is bribery. Another powerful example of God's 'rewards' and 'punishments' laid out for his Old Testament children is seen in Deuteronomy 28 where the Lord details a set of blessings contingent upon obedience (verses 1–14) and a set of curses for disobedience (verses 15–43). The Psalms abound in references to blessings on those who are obedient to their heavenly Father. One need go no further than the very first verse of the first Psalm to learn 'Blessed is the man who does not walk in the counsel of the wicked or stand in the way of sinners or sit in the seat of mockers.' Jesus picks up the refrain in the Beatitudes where he promises blessing to those who demonstrate certain qualities (Matt. 5:3–12). According to Hebrews 12:2, Jesus appears to use the hope of future joy as a motivation to endure the horror of the cross. This is not an exhaustive list, but it should suffice to show that there is biblical reason to include rewards in a system of discipline and not just punishments.

The Bible doesn't go much further than this in telling us specifically how to react to children's behaviour, though it is quite definite in advocating discipline that includes both positive and negative consequences. This leaves us to work out from these basics how we are to discipline our children and for what behaviour. I will share with you some strategies that have been proven by research and/or experience to be helpful.

Principles for managing children's behaviour

I will begin our discussion of practical ways to tame the 'folly' in the hearts of children with a few basic principles that are prerequisites to effective management of children's behaviour. (Once again, bear in mind that we are now focusing on a more narrow aspect of 'discipline' which assumes you are already working on the areas of teaching and character building covered earlier in this book.)

REWARD OR PUNISH CHILDREN BASED ON THEIR BEHAVIOUR, NOT YOUR FEELINGS

It is all too easy to let kids get away with some things when we are tired. It is also hard to be fair when they make us angry. Children should be able to tell we are upset when they disobey or otherwise sin, but the consequences should be for what they did, not for making us mad. God in his perfect holiness can execute his wrath because it is always fair and just. Our anger is often for selfish reasons and thus not a reliable guide to disciplining children. We do well to make clear that punishment is for the sin, not for getting us angry. Tempers often flare when parents give children multiple chances to obey but don't actually give them consequences. Children usually buy time until the parents, frustrated by the lack of response, become angry and thereby convince their offspring they mean business. This doesn't teach children their disobedience is wrong (for the parent did nothing about it over a number of chances), but that making mum or dad angry is. Children can learn quickly to read parents' moods to guide their behaviour, and this falls short of learning to do what is right for the right reason.

Parents who are frequently angry often reap what they sow as children learn to handle their frustrations in the same way. But their anger often is directed at their parents, prompting the parents in turn to rebuke and punish such disrespect. But here's the catch: respect comes more naturally when the parent acts in a respectable way. It is a challenge to respect someone with a bad temper. This also is a way to violate Paul's command to fathers not to exasperate their children (Eph. 6:4).

DETERMINE WHICH ACTIONS ARE WORTHY OF CONSEQUENCES

A major source of disagreement for parents is over which actions should meet with rewards or punishments. Here are some suggestions to help you decide.

1. Establish consequences for the character qualities you are trying to teach. This ties in to our earlier discussion about systematically teaching godly qualities. For example, if you are working on respect for adults, you might set up a programme to reward the child when they answer appropriately 'No, sir' or 'Yes, ma'am', punishing him for a failure to do so. If you are teaching gentleness, you might set up 'labs' where the child plays with his pet and is consciously trying to be gentle to earn a reward (such as decreased supervision of his time with the pet). When our daughter Erin was a pre-schooler, she was given a kitten and loved it dearly. She delighted in holding it, but the kitten quickly became uncomfortable in Erin's little arms. Erin didn't mean harm, but she put the cat through contortions that reminded me of a Chinese acrobat. Usually we were alerted to this situation by the doleful 'meow' of the cat seeking safety. My wife and I then set up a plan to teach Erin self-control and gentleness. If Erin did not pick up the cat without permission for several hours, she earned a taste of her favourite sweet. This meant we could supervise her handling of the cat and teach her to do so gently. The plan proved successful, and Erin and her cat continue to be good buddies.

2. Always have consequences for moral offences. I use this for lack of a better term, but I mean to include here behaviour that is clearly right or wrong according to Scripture. This would include lying, cursing, cheating and outright disobedience. I find it helpful to think in terms of morals, for it can increase agreement between parents. Parents rarely differ

on whether immoral acts should be punished, so making clear which behaviour falls into this category promotes unity.

3. Agree on a plan for non-moral behaviour. On the other hand, if something is not clearly a moral issue, then the parents are free to determine whether or not that behaviour is worth working on. Non-moral behaviour includes things such as eating everything on your plate, running in the house, bedtimes, curfews, or riding a bike to Mary's house. Obviously there is no Bible verse that says 'thou shalt be in bed by 8'. However, once a child's parents agree to draw such lines, they should be enforced as obedience issues. Family meetings can effectively be used to examine these areas and decide where the lines should be drawn. Children may have input on these (increasingly as they get older) but the parents have the final say. This enables children to learn discernment and develops relationships with parents.

ESTABLISH CLEAR RULES AS MUCH AS POSSIBLE

This follows from what we just said, for if a child's responsibility is not naturally clear (e.g. taking out the rubbish), then the parents do well to set a rule. Not only should the rules of the house be plain, but the consequences should be as well. Household policy can be tested by having someone else ask the child about a specific area (such as what time they are to be in the house in the evening). The child should be able to tell that person what is expected of her and what happens if she fails. Such clarity greatly aids the child's ability to control her own behaviour and abide by rules. I often explain this to children by observing how the police do us a favour by posting speed limits and making us aware that a ticket awaits if we transgress those limits.

ENFORCEMENT OF RULES SHOULD BE CONSISTENT ACROSS TIME AND PARENTS

If I speed, it doesn't matter whether it is Tuesday or Saturday, or whether Officer Smith or Officer Jones is on duty. I will get a ticket just the same. Consistently enforcing household rules helps the child learn that God's laws, too, are unchanging, and teaches her that efforts to manipulate the rules are doomed to failure. Rules and consequences are to be the same at any time and with either parent.

CONSIDER DIFFERENCES IN THE TEMPERAMENT OF CHILDREN

Research shows that nearly half of the personalities of children are due to temperament, inborn tendencies to act in certain ways. Many parents appreciate this after having one baby who was a breeze only to have their second-born challenge the frontiers of their patience. Parents have different temperaments, too. The match in temperaments between a particular parent and child is referred to as 'goodness of fit'. Sometimes the fit is good; other times it is not. A highly scheduled parent may have more conflict with an unscheduled child. A shy child may frustrate an outgoing mother. We could add many more examples, but the point is that the burden is on the parent to find a way of working with a child that suits his particular temperament.

To illustrate, consider a temperamentally anxious child who is eager to please her parents, but she has a brother who is impulsive and gets in trouble frequently for not thinking before acting. While the rules may need to be the same, the consequences parents use may have to differ. The boy in our story may need rather serious penalties to curb his impulses. But the girl will probably behave simply to avoid the disappointed look on her father's face. One size doesn't fit all when it comes to consequences.

MAKE EXPECTATIONS AND CONSEQUENCES APPROPRIATE FOR DIFFERENT AGES

Developmental psychologists tell us that children at different ages think in fundamentally different ways. For example, you can teach a pre-schooler the Golden Rule, but she probably won't be able to act on it for a few years. Why? Because she has not yet developed the mental ability to see a situation from someone else's perspective. Those working with children need to pay close attention to how those children think and make their expectations accordingly.

This also applies to consequences for behaviour. It seems that most pre-school children determine right or wrong largely on the basis of consequences alone. If you get punished for it, it is wrong. If you get praised, it is right. Primary-school-aged children tend toward more of a rule orientation, appealing to established policies to determine what is right. Teenagers develop the skills to reason about right and wrong in the way we do as adults. They can weigh options and draw their own conclusions. So, parents may do well to stress consequences to little ones, rules to primary school children, and decision-making skills to teens.

TEACH THE FIRST TIME, PUNISH THEREAFTER

Given that child-raising is an educational undertaking, it is reasonable to assume on most new offences that the child did not know better. For example, if your little girl plucks a flower from your garden to give to you as a gift, she might not realize that this could upset you. You would thank her for the thought and explain why those flowers aren't to be picked. I would suggest stating to her that the next time she does this, such and such will happen. If she doesn't catch on, and picks another flower knowingly, I would keep my promise about consequences.

This does not apply to offences that the child already knows to be wrong. You have taught your son repeatedly of the dangers of the road in front of your house and instructed him to stay in his garden. You give him some freedom in the garden and the next thing you know you spot him in the street. Here consequences should follow immediately because it was a wilful offence (not to mention a dangerous one).

ESTABLISH POSITIVE INCENTIVES FIRST

We tend to be quick to punish and slow to reward. This comes from the tendency to respond to transgressions instead of teaching positive behaviour. As employees, we wouldn't think much of a job where we were punished for poor performance but received no raises if we did a good job. It may be better, then, to set up rewards for the child's good behaviour in an area before establishing punishments. After all, we don't want to make the miniature golf mistake of setting a lot of boundaries while not directing our child to the goal of godly behaviour. Rewarding kindness, sharing, gentleness and obedience shows you value these and notice when your child behaves well. You can then add the negative to show the opposite results for failure. This helps the child to see that you want him to be good, not just to stay out of trouble.

PRIVILEGES AND RESPONSIBILITIES

Most of our adult life operates on the principle of earning privileges by demonstrating responsibility. My licence as a psychologist came after I fulfilled the set of requirements established by the state. It is now my privilege to practise as a psychologist unless I violate that privilege by being irresponsible in keeping the laws governing it. More appropriate for teens is the example of a driver's licence. You don't magically receive this sacred card in the post on your seventeenth birthday. The youth must also demonstrate responsibility in learning the laws and practising the skills. Once these are demonstrated, then the licence is given until such a time as it is abused and revoked.

Teenagers especially seem to respond to this type of reasoning by parents when it comes to non-moral privileges. These might include such things as how far from home one can drive, later curfews, shopping privileges, permission for special events, job opportunities, and certain purchases. Teens often bristle when their interests in such things are frustrated by parents who say they can have this privilege only when the parents 'feel' it is right. This causes two problems. First, it makes privileges seem arbitrary and deprives the young person of any sense of control in earning them. Second, deprived of control, the teen is likely to badger the parent in an effort to change their minds as she has no other recourse.

Part of our responsibility as Christian parents is to help our young ones learn to work to achieve goals, and here is an area where we can give them practise. If a privilege desired by a teen (or even younger child sometimes) is not sinful, then it is an issue of whether you can trust them to handle the privilege responsibly. If you are unsure, establish a set of requirements for the teen to earn that privilege, granting it when they are met. As you see, this works much like licensing, but this is also how job promotions are typically determined. Then, outline the 'rules' of the privilege, showing how it can be lost.

An example might be helpful. Rachel wants to be able to stay out until 11:30 on the weekends rather than 11:00, arguing this would give her time to get a hamburger with her friends after school sports events. However, Rachel has a history of being late anyway. Her parents might point this out, and say that she can earn the later curfew by being on time consistently for two months and being faithful to let her parents know where she is when away from home. Once these criteria are fulfilled, the later curfew is hers until she fails to be home on time or accurately report on her whereabouts. Working with privileges this way helps young people learn responsibility and to have a little more sense of control of their lives before they are out of the home and on their own for good.

Truth or consequences?

We now have a set of principles to guide our handling of children's behaviour. Let's get a little more specific, and discuss options for rewards and punishments.

We begin with a note of caution. Technically, rewards or punishments are defined by their effects on the child, not simply because you think they are rewarding or punishing. Consider licorice. This would be a reward for some of us, but for others the taste would be a punishment. It is a matter of individual preference. The same goes for consequences: be sure your child thinks your rewards are rewarding and your punishments punishing. I will offer a set of examples for the categories I describe below, and let you customize them for your children so that you are sure to use punishments the child dislikes and rewards that truly motivate. Also bear in mind that you may need to use different approaches with each of your children, and at different points in development.

POSITIVE INCENTIVES

This is simply the politically correct way to refer to rewards for desired behaviour. A major principle in using positive incentives is that the frequency decreases as children grow older while the potency increases. Pre-schoolers may need to earn rewards on an hourly basis if you are dealing with very frequent behaviour problems such as tantrums or going into siblings' rooms without permission. Primary rewards should be used with younger children. These are incentives that carry their worth with them immediately, like pieces of candy, raisins, or small toys or privileges. Secondary rewards, more appropriate after children begin school, are those which are meaningless in themselves but can be used for primary rewards. Money, for instance, is the favourite among secondary rewards. Having a few pennies or pounds doesn't do much for you, but take them to a shop and lots of exciting options abound. Tokens, tickets, or points are less frequently used but operate on the same principle. These are meaningless unless they can be 'cashed in' for something you have agreed to beforehand. As we saw above, privileges are fairly powerful rewards for teens. Earning a later curfew or increased driving privileges will motivate many young people eager to gain greater independence.

One useful idea with secondary reinforcements or rewards is to have them cashed in to earn activities that we may currently give our children 'free of charge'. These include outdoor privileges, television or video access, or telephone time. You might arrange it so each half-hour of approved television costs 25 pence or 5 points which are earned by doing jobs without prompting or by using good manners at dinner.

A simpler way to do the same thing is to have children earn after-school privileges by their behaviour during the day. This avoids the details of tokens and the like and puts privileges back into the category of things children earn for being good and not things that are their natural rights. It is not considered child abuse if a boy or girl is deprived of cartoons or access to their collection of toys.

The number one reason that positive incentive systems fail is because the rewards take too long to get. Little children are more controlled by the immediate situation than the prospect of getting something in a week or a month. Even if Johnny wants to go to his favourite fast-food establishment, it won't motivate his present behaviour if it is too far in the future. This is why paying children for good grades often doesn't help too much. Six or nine weeks away is a long time. If you are providing incentives for school performance, it is better to do it on a daily or weekly basis until children mature a bit.

I would be remiss if I failed to mention the value of verbal 'rewards', also known as praise. As believers, we all hope to hear from our Lord, 'Well done, good and faithful servant', and why would it be otherwise with our children? I don't know any adults who are indifferent to a 'well done' during the day, and certainly children as a rule enjoy hearing they have pleased their parents. Some children are not receptive to praise when there are problems in the parent–child relationship, but affirmation and encouragement are generally powerful motivators.

PRIVILEGE LOSS

This is a first cousin of the plan we have just described, having one minor difference. Here the child already has the privileges in the 'bank' but can lose them if he does not behave as expected. Johnny may leave for school knowing he has a full hour to play in the garden after school provided he brings home his homework and cleans his room. If he fails, he loses his privilege. You can do the same thing with allowance or point systems. Your child can plan on getting his allowance on Saturday, but can be fined for certain offences during the week.

The most popular form of privilege loss is grounding, a favourite among parents of teenagers. This refers to varying levels of losing the right to such teen addictions as telephone talking or weekend socializing. This typically works fairly well, but sometimes is ineffective because the parents don't follow through on enforcing the limits. Often this is due to parents grounding their children for huge periods of time that cannot realistically be enforced. I recommend short, hard groundings. Take all privileges for a period of a day or two. This is more easily enforced and doesn't demoralize the teen in the process. I have met a number of adolescents who were depressed because they were on a very long period of grounding. This is also ineffective in behaviour change because the child feels stuck: even if she is good for weeks, she will still be grounded. So, why try? Shorter, more severe groundings alleviate this problem.

PUNISHMENT

Let's look at several unpleasant consequences that might be used to influence children when they transgress limits.

Logical consequences. This refers to thinking up a 'punishment' that fits the specific crime. If Josh tracks mud on the floor, he should clean it up. If Annie leaves the milk out, the new gallon comes from her allowance. You probably get the idea. Using logical consequences takes some creative energy, but they are helpful and practical tools for teaching good behaviour.

Time out. You guessed this would be in here, didn't you? Actually, time out is not really a punishment, but a specific type of privilege loss. It is a little child's version of being grounded from the fun activities in the home. Time out can be a useful tool for the parent if used correctly. Let's begin with a variant for little ones. 'Baby time-outs' are helpful once children can crawl. Here one picks up the child abruptly and sits him down in another part of the room, facing away from whatever mischief he had found. A firm 'No!' should accompany this gesture.

More traditional types of time outs can be used for toddlers. The concept is to punish the child by boring her, removing her from any interesting activity. A chair in the corner of an unpopular room is best (dining rooms seem to work fairly well), and the child is placed there for a period of one minute per year of life. That is, a five-year-old sits for five minutes, and an eight-year-old sits for eight. The key is that both child and parent need to be quiet during this time. If you interact with your child, your punishment may be seen as a reward to the child who now has your attention. (Remember our 'licorice' example earlier?) Many children will take such negative attention over no attention. The time should not start until the child is quiet. If the child gets out of the chair or persists in arguing about the time out, then a spanking is in order. The spanking is punishment for not taking the time out, so the time out still must be served after the spanking.

A variant on time out is the sending of the child to her room. This is less popular because these days many children's rooms are cornucopias of entertainment. This might be more successful if children were sent to the dining room or another less amusing place.

Other punishments. Parents through the ages have been quite creative in developing punishments, and we certainly won't exhaust the options here. Just take care that the punishment fits the crime and is not abusive. Writing sentences such as 'I will not lie about my homework' numerous times is a common option, but I discourage this. We want children to enjoy writing and it seems to be a conflicting message if we teach them that writing is punishment. I also do not generally encourage military types of punishment including exercises, standing in painful postures, and the like as these can easily be physically harmful to the child.

Extra chores are a popular choice and this has merit. Work penalties for certain offences can be effective and can be meted out either by task (clean the bathroom) or by unit of time (one hour of chores per offence). This still carries the implication that work is punishment which may conflict with Genesis 3:17 where Adam was commissioned to work in the garden before he sinned. However, Genesis 3:17–19 suggests work became burdensome after the Fall. One handy way to use this notion is to punish a child who offends a sibling by having him perform the sibling's regular chores for a period of time.

Spanking. Let me propose a few guidelines for corporal punishment since we have already demonstrated that this is a biblical option. Care should be taken to use corporal punishment at appropriate ages. Formal spankings are probably not helpful for infants but a swat on the hand that reaches for the electrical outlet can communicate danger. (After all, God gave us pain to warn us of danger, and so it is with spankings.) Children begin to outgrow spankings by middle school, depending on the size of the child and parent.

First, establish clear rules so your child knows what behaviour will earn a spanking. Major offences, such as lying, merit spankings immediately. Otherwise, spankings are good as second level consequences if the child does not cooperate with the initial punishment. We saw this in the time-out plan above. The concern here is that a spanking is the 'nuclear bomb' of the parenting arsenal. It should not be used for minor infractions, so you keep the option of increasing the stakes should the child resist the milder punishment.

Second, control yourself when you spank. If you are angry, delay the spanking until you can punish the misbehaviour and not take personal revenge. Respect the possibility that you, too, can err when you punish your child.

Third, have a planned method for spanking. I discourage canes and belts because of the high risk of leaving marks on the child. A wooden spoon or a paddle stings and, because it is broad and flat, is unlikely to leave injuries. Before you spank, determine the number of 'swats'. A large number rarely accomplishes more 'education' than a couple, and may provoke bitterness on the part of the child. Both you and the child should be aware of this limit before the sentence is executed.

Fourth, don't chase the child through the house before or during the spanking. (A little girl once told me how she loved to be spanked because her mum had to chase her for an hour to catch her. She felt the pain of the spanking was a fair price for the hour's entertainment.) Spank in a specified place. This avoids the game-playing that some children make out of a spanking while building in a safety system to insure you are not swatting impulsively.

Finally, review with the child why he was spanked and discuss how repeats can be avoided. Many parents find it meaningful to pray with their child after spanking them. This may be all right, but make sure the child is ready to pray and doesn't misunderstand the meaning of the gesture.

With any of these disciplinary strategies, seek God in prayer and consult with your mate because this is such a vital part of your ministry as a parent. Fairness and control should always characterize Christian parents when managing the behaviour of their children. As we have seen, there is no set formula for 'how to' discipline our children because the Bible doesn't offer one and because we must appreciate the differences among our children. This leaves each set of parents, or the single parent in homes where the marriage has failed, to develop a plan for their particular children. Don't hesitate to seek counsel from a pastor or other respected believer to help you develop your plan. God grant us wisdom to be faithful in disciplining our children in a way that teaches without exasperating.

8

TEACHING CHILDREN
TO HONOUR THEIR PARENTS

*'Honour your father and your mother, so that you may live long
in the land the* LORD *your God is giving you'* (Exod. 20:12).

*'We should look up to those who God has placed over us, and
should treat them with honour, obedience, and gratefulness.
It follows from this that we are forbidden to detract from their
dignity either by contempt, or stubbornness, or by ungratefulness'*
(John Calvin).

Having at this point in my life successfully communicated to
my daughter what I consider a fun night out, Erin will eagerly
ask on Friday nights, 'Can we go to a bookshop?' Not wanting
to disappoint her (nor myself, nor my wife—addiction can run
in families), we grant her request and off we go. She generally
gathers up a few books and settles into a comfortable spot to read.
Occasionally I wander through the children's section where
she landed, and survey the titles. All manner of books can be
found on almost any topic, customized to the limited literacy of
children.

What I have never found is a children's book on how to be
a better son or daughter. After all, adults read books on Christian
parenting, and have dozens to choose from. But our children don't

follow our lead. Can you imagine James Dobson reworking his best-seller for children, making it *Dare to Accept Discipline*? Do you think a book like *Building Your Mum and Dad's Self-Esteem by Being Obedient* would make a best-seller list? I doubt it.

Children seem to have less intrinsic motivation to be obedient than parents do to be obeyed. Chalk it up to original sin, and children's natural self-centredness. Yet, God reserved one of his Ten Commandments to address children's attitudes toward parents. He anticipated the problem, and wanted it to be clear that children should honour their parents. Strangely, if we want our children to be fully obedient to God, then we will long for them to honour us. This is not for selfish reasons, however, but because such honour reveals that the child is grasping his or her place in God's chain of authority.

Additionally, this is important for us because we have the opportunity to demonstrate such honour as our children witness our interactions with our parents. We easily fail to notice that this command doesn't expire when one becomes an adult.

Therefore, I want us to look at the fifth commandment and what it entails. I will then offer some suggestions as to how we can support our children's obedience to it. In doing so, I will use the themes presented by the pastor/theologian John Calvin as detailed in his *Institutes of the Christian Religion*.[1]

The quote at the beginning of this chapter captures the three aspects of honouring parents that Calvin stresses. We will consider each of these in turn.

Regarding parents with reverence

To honour is to revere, to view as having great dignity. We have learned that having children means we are blessed by God, given little ones as his gracious gifts. Children then owe honour to their parents by virtue of their position as parents, just as we are to hold our leaders in esteem (Rom. 13:1–7) because of their position in God's structure of authority. The point here is that we are to esteem parents highly even if they are grossly flawed, because the value comes from the title, not the performance.

Revering parents is obviously easier if they appear worthy of the honour. The godly woman of Proverbs 31 is called 'blessed' by her children (v. 28) because of her diligence. Fathers merit the respect of their children because of their faithful discipline (Heb. 12:9). These are only two examples of the honour of children being a response to virtue in their parents.

It is easy for us to complain about our parents in front of our children, belittling their finicky ways as they age. We must be aware that in so doing we may sabotage our children's respect for us. Again, parents are to be honoured by virtue of their position and not their performance, and this holds true for our parents as well. Leviticus 19:32 instructs us to 'rise in the presence of the aged, show respect for the elderly and revere your God'. Prayerfully consider whether you expect more honour from your children than they see you show to your parents.

If we pursue the ideals of godly character outlined in Chapter 5, we make our children's responsibility to honour us an easier one. As noted in Hebrews 12:9, using fair and reasonable discipline also encourages honour from our children.

The trick to this, however, is that reverence cannot be forced. I have often told parents that Adolf Hitler commanded obedience, but did not always get respect. Many people obeyed him out of slavish fear alone and not because of their admiration of him. In a similar manner, we can have obedient children who still do not respect us, and we cannot force them to do so. We must strive to be respectable, but must rely on the Holy Spirit to teach them to honour us.

Obeying parents

The second aspect of honouring parents, according to Calvin, is obedience. We discussed ways to try to encourage it in Chapter 7, but here our focus is having our children obey from their hearts out of honour for us.

We now come to examine Paul's admonition to children in the 'family section' of Ephesians, the central verses being 6:1–3:

> Children, obey your parents in the Lord, for this is right. 'Honour your father and mother' — which is the first commandment with a promise — 'that it may go well with you and that you may enjoy long life on the earth.'

Verse 1 is echoed in Colossians 3:20, with the added note that children are to obey parents 'in everything' and with the added motive, 'for this pleases the Lord.'

Paul thus implies that obedience is a part of honouring parents. Such obedience is to be 'in the Lord' and 'in everything'. If we collapse these two categories, we see that children are to obey their parents in all things that are consistent with God's nature. This means that unless they are asked to sin, they are to obey. It is crucial that children be taught this. Especially as they move toward adolescence, there is a tendency for children to weigh the 'fairness' of a parental expectation. If they think it is fair, they obey (usually). If not, they may argue their point. While it is appropriate for parents to explain their expectations to children, agreement is not the basis of obedience. The God-ordained structure of authority is.

Calvin adds that children should obey even if parents are unfair and exhibit what he calls 'immoderate strictness', so long as what they are requiring is lawful. This type of thinking doesn't play well with today's youth, but I doubt that it was ever very popular. Many aspects of the Christian life aren't popular, such as self-control, sacrifice and suffering, to name only a few. This is why it is so important to cultivate in our children a desire to please God. Obedience with resentment will not fulfil the command, and we want to lead our offspring to a fervent motivation to please God, even when it is uncomfortable. Here is where teaching them the greatness of God is important. It increases the desire to obey as we realize the majesty of God and the marvellous things he has done for us. Further incentive is found in knowing that Jesus, the perfect God–Man, obeyed his earthly parents (Luke 2:51), which required greater submission than any children today will have to muster.

Learning to obey out of principle makes much sense in light of the task of preparing children for the 'real world' of adulthood. Teenagers taking their first jobs will not be expected to judge what work they think is reasonable, but to do what is told them without question. This will hold true throughout their lives.

I should add a note on the caveat that obedience is not required when parents usurp God's authority to ask children to do something contrary to his law. The authority of parents is an extension of God's, so to tell children to go against his will is to commit insubordination. In the armed forces, if a general has given you a command and a lower officer tells you differently, your responsibility is to obey the general. So it is with parents in God's hierarchy of command.

Obedience begins with listening to parents, an action commanded in Proverbs 1:8 as the prerequisite to wisdom and obedience. One must know what parents expect before one can do it. As parents, it is our responsibility to make our expectations clear, and to monitor our children to see that they indeed listen. Problems with this basic communication are found in many families. Children, on the other hand, need to be tuned in to parents when they give instruction, and this will be more natural when they are eager to please God and their parents. (As you can see, positive motivation gets better results than fear of retribution. God, too, is more pleased with us when we obey out of love than out of fear of consequences.)

Children are to heed discipline, as is stressed in Proverbs 15:5, 32; 16:20; 23:22. And, they can be obedient. It can be observed in their character by others (Prov. 20:11). It can be exhibited at an early age. Josiah (2 Kings 22:1–2) at eight years of age was known to do what was right in the eyes of the Lord. Let us not set expectations for our children that are too low, but encourage them toward lives of consistent obedience.

Gratitude toward parents

Jesus illustrated the virtue of gratitude in his healing of the ten men with leprosy in Luke 17:11–19, showing his displeasure at the nine who received healing but didn't take the time to thank him. Parenting can be a ministry that receives little thanks, or as I sometimes put it, one where you get little change back from your investment. This is truer in the short run than over time.

Mark Twain once said, 'When I was a boy of fourteen, my father was so ignorant I could hardly stand to have the man around. But when I got to be twenty-one, I was astonished at how much he had learnt in seven years.' Maturity, and especially having children of your own, has a way of making you more appreciative of what your parents went through. Children easily overlook the sacrifice and wisdom of their parents. But they may fail to learn gratitude partly from lacking adequate opportunity to see it in action.

Paul, in 1 Timothy 5:4, tells us, 'But if a widow has children or grandchildren, these should learn first of all to put their religion into practice by caring for their own family and so repaying their parents and grandparents, for this is pleasing to God.' Caring for our parents is seen here as a form of gratitude for all we received from them. We must examine ourselves at this point. Like Twain, we are in a better position to appreciate what they have done than our children are to appreciate our efforts.

This still is no excuse for our children. They are to be grateful. There are some developmental constraints, for gratitude to a degree requires the ability to see the way things could have been worse and aren't. For example, young children may assume their family is no different from others until they learn of the angry outbursts their peers receive from their parents. It is thus our task to point out how God has blessed us in contrast to what we as sinners deserve. Practical activities, such as writing 'Thank you' notes and listing blessings, can help teach gratitude.

A command with consequences

Paul observes that the fifth commandment is the first command-ment with a promise, thereby pointing children to the benefits of honouring parents. There are three mentioned in Scripture, and I encourage you to bring them to the attention of your children.

LONG LIFE

This is seen in Exodus 20:12 and reiterated in Ephesians 6:3. By this is meant a life of blessedness, a lengthier time of earthly fellowship as prelude to our eternal bliss with God. A key word here is 'enjoy', for the attitude of honouring comes from a life focused on God and which has thus entered into his pleasures.

THINGS GOING WELL

Paul also refers to the blessing of things going well with those who keep the command, drawing this from Deuteronomy 5:16. In Deuteronomy, the going well refers to life in the Promised Land, but that was not directly relevant to the Ephesians. Rather, a life of blessedness is promised wherever you are on the earth. As with the Beatitudes, this blessedness may be more spiritual than material, but after all, that is the better of the two anyway.

PLEASING GOD

Few things excite us quite like feeling we have pleased a loved one. Observe the pure delight on the parents' faces on Christmas morning when their child opens a gift they have carefully selected and jumps with joy. It is difficult to tell whether the parent or the child is happier. When you love someone, one of your greatest pleasures is knowing you have pleased them.

So when Paul relates in Colossians 3:20 that God is pleased by the obeying of parents, the genuine Christian discovers a powerful motive for obedience. Again, we need first to apply this to our treatment of our parents for, as we saw in 1 Timothy 5:4, this is to be the motive of adult children, too. As for our children, as God works in their hearts a fervent desire to please him, they will revel in knowing that their obedience to us has the added benefit of pleasing God.

THE CONSEQUENCES OF DISHONOURING PARENTS

If God rewards those who honour their parents, it follows that failing in this will bring negative consequences.

Disobedience would mean the opposite of the blessings. This implies the shortening of life, a loss of joy in life going well, and displeasing God. In short, a disobedient child is cursed (Deut. 27:16). For the Christian, these are not pleasant thoughts. But in Israel dishonouring one's parents met with more immediate consequences. Deuteronomy 21:18–21 gives the procedure for dealing with a rebellious son who disobeys his parents and does not listen to them. He was to be presented to the elders and stoned to death. Attacking or cursing parents was also a capital offence (Exod. 21:15, 17). Severe consequences for sure, but these make clear the seriousness of God about the honour of parents.

Disobedient children can also be signs of broader judgment by God. Rebellious children are seen as signs of apostasy in Micah 7:6. As Paul describes the withdrawing of God's restraining hand from the sinful world in Romans 1, we witness the mushrooming of sin. Tucked into the litany of evils in the last part of this chapter we find the phrase 'they disobey their parents' (Rom. 1:30). Children need to know the seriousness of disobedience as it can be symptomatic of a broadly sinful life.

Beyond our parents

Malachi 1:6 suggests that honouring our parents is a form of honouring God, for it is the most basic place where we demonstrate submission to authority. This points to deferring to the authority of teachers, employers, rulers (Prov. 24:21), church leadership (1 Tim. 5:17), and all who are placed over us by God. This submissive attitude stands in dramatic relief against the backdrop of self-assertion that characterizes our day, but it is one that we are to exhibit. It is also an attitude that we are to teach to our children, and prayerfully to expect.

Helping children to honour parents

Teaching children to honour their parents is tricky. As I mentioned about Hitler earlier, we can force obedience but respect must come from the heart. We must then promote an honouring attitude, but it cannot ultimately be demanded directly. It comes from a heart that seeks to please God and us as parents. There are some things we can do, however, and I will reiterate these as we conclude.

HONOUR OUR HEAVENLY FATHER IN OUR LIVES

This harks back to Chapter 5, but its importance cannot be overly stressed. It is difficult to ask of our children something they cannot see modelled in our lives. Our dealings with God and authorities over us provide concrete examples that our children can follow. Our adherence to the broader implications of honouring authority is a life-long responsibility.

HONOUR OUR PARENTS

There is no age limit on the fifth commandment, so we are responsible to show reverence toward our parents as long as they live. We do this in the way we speak about our parents, help them with their needs, pray for them, and care for them as they age. Our children benefit from joining us as we visit their grandparents, assisting us in caring for those who have given so much to us.

TEACH CHILDREN THE IMPORTANCE OF RESPECT

It is easy to assume children understand that they should respect us as their parents. But don't take it for granted. Lovingly (*not critically*) review the outline of this chapter with them. Use family worship or Bible study to dig deeper into the Scriptures on the topic. Talk to them about it when things are calm. Saying 'You're supposed to respect me!' in the heat of an argument probably won't accomplish what you desire.

Try simply asking your children why they should obey you. Their answers will give you a measure of their understanding of the subject. You can move from there to explain the biblical reasons, with the benefits and consequences that accompany obedience and disobedience.

BE REASONABLE

Though children are to respect parents so long as they are requiring what God requires, this comes easier when they view their parents as fair and reasonable. Seek the counsel of friends on the ways you handle misbehaviour, and on how they see you as coming across to your children in your attitudes: 'a wise man listens to advice' (Prov. 12:15b). For example, ask a friend whether they think your response to a particular situation was fair and reasonable.

PRAY FOR YOUR CHILDREN

We learned that honour for parents is not for your sake primarily, but for God's. It is not selfish to yearn for your children to possess this quality of righteousness, even though it is to your benefit also. Just beware your motives. The goal is for your children to please God, not to make your task as a parent easier. (Though that's not a bad side effect!)

Children who honour their parents honour God as well. They become conspicuous in a self-assertive world of disrespectful children (and adults). I know as a counsellor, it is most refreshing to talk with children who speak well of parents rather than complain about them. Pursue respect from your children to the glory of God and the furtherance of His kingdom.

9

WHERE DO CHILDREN
FIT IN THE CHURCH?

'The promise is for you and your children' (Acts 2:39a).

'Let the little children come to me, and do not hinder them, for the kingdom of heaven belongs to such as these' (Matt. 19:14).

Like most people, my wife and I enjoy eating out. However, after our daughter was born, this became more of an adventure, especially when we were on vacation. We would go to new restaurants and feel a sense of dread as we entered. The suspense would build up until we opened the door and saw balloons ready to be given to young diners. Our anxiety would continue to ease if our hostess reached for a children's menu and some crayons to help our tike pass the time till her food arrived. In such places, she was welcome, and we were glad. On another occasion, though, things didn't go so well. The anxious beating of my heart accelerated as the door opened and I heard quiet piano music. The host looked at us with an air of condescension and asked, 'A table for how many?' No children's menu. No crayons. Just a number of people without children staring, almost daring our daughter to make a noise. She usually obliged.

Visiting churches can be like going to restaurants. You may not be sure where (and sometimes whether) your children will belong. It all depends on the particular church. Some feel children distract from worship, others figure they get little out of it, and still others want families to worship together. Some churches simply haven't given it much thought.

Part of the problem is that many churches lack an understanding of where children fit into the body of Christ. This is by no means to say that they don't care about children, but it is to say few churches have a good idea of the place of children in the overall functioning of the congregation.

Having looked closely at the nurture of children in families, we turn now to their place in the church and to consider its responsibilities to children. The role of the church in the lives of the children in her midst is major, and one that has been regrettably neglected. I agree with Rodney Clapp who reminds us, 'The family is not God's most important institution on earth … The church is.'[1] Children need to know their place in the Bride of Christ. I believe the confusion here is largely due to the lack of a clear theological understanding of the matter. Children in the church force us to address issues that are controversial, and we have a tendency to avoid such difficult topics. Yet, if we are to be true to our calling in the lives of little ones, we need to address these matters. And that is what we shall do in this and the following three chapters.

Our first task is to consider the place children have within the body of Christ. We will approach this from two perspectives. First we will look at the things to be learned from Jesus' interactions with children and the place they held in his earthly ministry. We will then look directly at the scriptural teachings about the place of children in the worshipping community.

Children in Jesus' life and teachings

Children were a priority in Jesus' ministry. William Hendriksen lists the following references (based in Matthew and noting parallel passages in the other gospels) to demonstrate how frequently children were around Jesus: Matthew 14:21; 15:38; 18:3; 19:13–14 (cp. Mark. 10:13–14; Luke 18:15–16); 21:15–16; in a sense, 23:37 (cp. Luke 13:34).[2] It seems Matthew sought to make Jesus' interest in children a particular focus, so we will base our study in his Gospel.

HUMBLE AS A CHILD

In Matthew 18:1–4, Jesus responds to the disciples' arguing over who is the greatest in the kingdom with an object lesson, setting a child in their midst. Entrance into the kingdom, he explains, depends on conversion and becoming like a child. In contrast to the common devaluing of children in his day, our Lord makes a point of using a child as an example. A child was likely chosen because of the humility his low estate would engender. Humility is a virtue throughout the Bible and one that is dramatically contrary to our culture. While children today should feel secure and loved, parents are still called to instil humility in their offspring. Jesus' disciples were to change their hearts and become humble like a child if they wanted to achieve kingdom greatness.

If our Saviour paid special attention to humble children, how important it is for us to follow him in this. Children of today's Christians will form the bulk of the members of the church in years to come. They should be a priority in the considerations of the leadership of our churches. Let us not overlook these precious gifts God has given to us.

ON NOT CAUSING CHILDREN TO STUMBLE

Jesus continues in Matthew 18:5–6 to describe the care such little ones require. They should not be taken advantage of nor caused to stumble. In contrast to the disciples' power-seeking, they are to attend to the humble. This most likely relates to adults, but it seems reasonable to imply that believing children, or children of believers, exemplifying this quality, should receive similar treatment, especially as Jesus did not exclude the literal child in their midst as an object of his teaching.

The principle is clear: we are to exhibit humility by showing compassion towards those not esteemed by the world. For our present purposes, this means children. Here is a call to reach out to the children in our congregations in loving ministry. This should go beyond 'Christian education' and evangelism, to meet the needs of those hurt by the divorce of their parents, physical or emotional illness, or financial hardship. Our reach should continue into the community to the children who are suffering there from poverty, neglect, abuse and other ills that haunt our society. This is illustrated in my town by a group establishing private Christian schools for poor inner-city children. The world needs to see the church take a lead in efforts to care for the needy children of our world. Our text says that it would be better to die than to cause these little ones to stumble. The challenge is issued. Would to God that we take this warning to heart!

THE ANGELS OF LITTLE ONES

Another reason not to despise such little ones is, 'their angels in heaven always see the face of my Father in heaven' (Matt. 18:10). While there is reason to believe Jesus is speaking of believers in general, he also seems to include children in this admonition. Hendriksen is confident that 'the little children are included, to be sure!'[3] Matthew Henry sees this as referring to the covenant children of Christians and notes, 'The infant seed of the faithful belong to the family of Christ, and are not to be despised.'[4]

In our day angels are such a popular topic, and are quite misunderstood, so we need to see that this probably does not provide proof of 'guardian angels'. Rather, the notion is that children are watched over by legions of angels, this idea being supported by Psalm 91:11 and Hebrews 1:14. The point of this reference is that, as John Calvin tells us, 'It is no light matter to despise those who have angels for their companions and friends, to take vengeance in their behalf.'[5] The teaching is that, vulnerable though children may be, they are well armed with a host of angels for defence against those who would despise them. Here is comfort far greater than the notion of a single guardian angel. Obviously God places great value on these little ones, providing them with angelic protection. God's people also are to accept and protect the little ones.

OF SUCH IS THE KINGDOM

Later (Matt. 19:13–15; cp. Mark 10:13–16 and Luke 18:15–17), some parents brought some children to Jesus for him to lay hands on them and pray. It was customary for Jewish parents in that time to take children to rabbis for blessings. The disciples, still missing the point, rebuke them. Jesus indignantly retorts, 'Let the children come to me, and do not hinder them; for the kingdom of heaven belongs to such as these.' Or, as the King James more poetically states it, 'Of such is the kingdom.' Jesus then proceeds to lay hands on the children, even touchingly taking them in his arms (Mark 10:16).

There is an impressive degree of unanimity among major commentators that Jesus here includes literal children. Spurgeon states it clearly, 'I am not inclined to get away from the plain sense of that expression, nor to suggest that he merely means that the kingdom consists of those who are like children. It is clear that he intended such children as those who were before him—babes and young children.'[6]

Children form part of the kingdom of God. This truth is firmly established by Jesus and, though specifics may be debated, is in its essence incontrovertible. Here is further reason for valuing children, and including them within the church's ministry. They are an integral part of the kingdom Christ has established and is building, a process in which we are to play a part. We must make these little ones a priority and understand their part in Christ's kingdom. We cannot see them as an inconvenience, a distraction, or a bother.

It is noteworthy that these parents had also requested prayer for their children, but the Gospel accounts do not say Jesus prayed for the children. This possibly reflects that Jesus, being God himself, did not need to appeal to the Father for such a blessing. He gave it himself.

We should observe two things about these children. First, there is no indication that they were sick or dying, so the blessing being sought was not a physical one. Second, Calvin observes that Jesus received those obviously too young to know their need.[7] These infants were absolutely passive in receiving the blessing. The only faith involved here was that of the parents who brought their children to Jesus. We thereby establish that Jesus honours parents' wishes for his blessing on their young children, independent of the children's will or faith.

What, though, was the meaning of such a blessing? This has been a subject of considerable debate. Dogmatic conclusions as to exactly what made these children members of the kingdom are inappropriate, but it is clear that the spiritual blessing of Jesus must either affirm their kingdom status or cause it. Either way, Jesus' blessing demonstrates his bringing children into his kingdom, independent of their overt profession of faith.

This suggests to me that children need to be considered as part of the church in some sense. It would be strange to have members of God's kingdom excluded from his visible people. They have a place and they belong. If children are to be considered as part of the community of faith, how does that impact our operations as churches? In what ways do we marginalize children in our activities? How might we include them more in our ministries? Might we even listen to them and see what suggestions they might have?

If children are part of the kingdom, exactly how are we to understand this? The covenant of God give us insight to answer this question.

Children of the Covenant

Traditions that see baptism as saving children consider them members of the church from that point on. Churches that expect a conversion experience see them as outside the body of believers until they are saved, and so they are proper subjects of evangelism. Covenant theology considers them to be members of the covenant community and participants in its blessings, but not fully so until they demonstrate faith and are admitted to the Lord's table. Let's try to understand this better.

We first encountered the idea of covenant children in chapter four with regard to whether children dying in infancy can be saved. We learned that God typically worked with families when he made covenants, indicating that the children of believing parents stood in a special relationship to him. We now need to broaden this to show how these families are joined together in the broader body of Christ.

Genesis uses its first eleven chapters to set the background for God's great plan of salvation. We learn of the fall of man and early culture where godly individuals rapidly became anomalies, and sin led to judgment with the flood and at Babel. With it sufficiently clear that humanity is fallen, God inaugurates his gracious plan of salvation by faith with Abram. Chapters 12–16 communicate the wonderful interactions of God with his servant, God directing and promising while Abram responds (usually) in faith.

Genesis 17 depicts God formalizing his covenant with His servant, now named Abraham, to reflect the wonderful promises of God. God speaks in verse 7, 'I will establish my covenant as an everlasting covenant between me and you and your descendants after you for the generations to come, to be your God and the God of your descendants after you.' As the text proceeds, we learn that Abraham was to keep the covenant and doing so included circumcising every male in his entourage (verses 9–14).

Several aspects of this covenant are critical for our purposes. First, God's covenant with Abraham is everlasting, not terminating with the coming of Jesus. Second, it applied not only to Abraham but also to his children (indeed, having numerous descendants was very much a part of God's promise to Abraham). Third, this covenant was to be signified by circumcision that was administered to that offspring (as well as to others within his household). Then in Hebrews 11:8–12 we have stated forthrightly that the responsibility of Abraham in this covenant was faith (also supplied by God). We should also note that the covenant was established through the line of Isaac (Gen. 17:21) but circumcision was applied to Ishmael the same day that God made the covenant (v. 23), showing that the sign applied to all of Abraham's offspring, chosen or not.

As God's promise was fulfilled and Abraham's offspring multiplied, the rite of circumcision of the male children continued. It was directly commanded of the people of Israel in Leviticus 12:3 while Deuteronomy 10:16 makes clear that the heart was the most important object of circumcision. In Deuteronomy 30:6 God promises his people that he will circumcise their hearts and the hearts of their descendants himself.

We thus understand that circumcision was a sign of grace administered to infants in the Old Testament, despite their being mentally incapable of comprehending its meaning, and despite their sometimes not growing into the 'circumcision of the heart', sharing in the true faith of Abraham. We noted this with

Ishmael's circumcision, and we see it again in Malachi 1:2–3 and Romans 9:10–13 where Esau, though circumcised, was doomed from the beginning to be outside the faith of the covenant.

This reveals that there were two groups in Israel, the 'visible church' consisting of those who had been circumcised and their families, regardless of whether they lived daily by faith, and the 'invisible church' of the true children of the covenant. American theologian Charles Hodge concludes that young children were thus members of the Old Testament church community.[8] He anticipates the possible objection that they were merely members of the civil community by reminding us that this distinction was not made in the days of Israel's theocracy.

Does the same principle apply to God's people in the era of the church? Does God continue his covenant promises to children born to his faithful, or were children born to Israel blessed in a way ours are not? God's Word offers a fully adequate answer.

In Romans 11 Paul develops the metaphor of the Gentiles being cut from a wild olive tree and grafted into a cultivated olive tree which had had some of its branches removed. The meaning is clear: Gentile believers become a part of a people whose 'roots' are with the Jewish people of God in the Old Testament. Far from dissecting the two peoples, Paul takes great care to show how Gentile believers of the New Testament are of one faith (and one covenant) with the Jewish faithful from the Old.

Paul approaches this issue again in a more directly doctrinal section, Ephesians 2:11–22. Writing to Gentiles, the apostle notes that they were formerly called the 'Uncircumcised' (v. 11) and were 'foreigners to the covenants of the promise' (v. 12), but have now been brought near by Christ. 'Consequently, you are no longer foreigners and aliens, but fellow-citizens with God's people and members of God's household' (v. 19). In Galatians 3:29 Paul proclaims, 'If you belong to Christ, then you are Abraham's seed, and heirs according to the promise.'

The point is sealed by the apostle Peter in his first epistle (2:9–10) as he borrows titles for God's people from the Old Testament ('chosen people...royal priesthood...holy nation... a people belonging to God') and applies them to Christians who were formerly 'not a people'. In so doing Peter joins with the other testimony of Scripture in affirming that the people of God are one throughout history, all being his through the covenant of grace, being saved by faith.

If Christians today share the same promise, then we are a special community of faith. As the sign of the promise was given to children in Israel, so our children are included as well. We will see in the next chapter how this helps us to understand baptism and the Lord's Supper, but our point for now is that our children are heirs to the promise. Though the promise was always to those who share Abraham's faith, the sign of the covenant, and inclusion in the covenant community, belong to the children of believers. Our children are part of the visible church, and are to be treated as members of the community of faith. They are the heirs apparent to the promised blessing, though we nurture them to grow into the faith of Abraham to claim their blessed inheritance.

Implications for churches and families

Where, then, do children fit into our churches? As an integral part of who we are. They are not outsiders, but a part of the church family as much as of our own. They are not to be overlooked or shoved to the periphery. They are part of God's kingdom and recipients of his blessing. They are heirs to the wonderful promise of God, and share in our joys of being his people. We dare not in any way hinder them from receiving the blessing of Jesus.

As an integral part of the community of faith, children are to be part of our worship. (More on this in Chapter 11.) They should be prayed for and ministered to by pastors and church leadership. We should make a concerted effort to nurture their faith and to join with families is raising them to be godly. They should be valued in our Christian education plans and efforts.

I would like to make a few specific suggestions. First, I urge men of the church to consider teaching children in Sunday school. Somehow this frequently is seen as women's work. But the example of godly men is of great worth to little ones, and teenagers, too.

I urge pastors and church leadership to get to know the children in their congregation, even though someone may be designated to minister to children. Pray for them by name. Get pictures of them to help you keep their names straight. Make them a priority. A special memory of my daughter's is of our pastor 'stopping traffic' in his receiving line after a Sunday sermon so that he could pray for her sore throat. A minor gesture, but one that made a lasting memory on a child.

I encourage those working with children and youth to explore creative ways to involve children in ministry. I caught the youth at our church going to the parking lot during their midweek meeting and washing the windows of the cars, leaving notes saying this had been done to the glory of God. Take children to visit hospitals or nursing homes. Have them adopt missionaries, praying for and corresponding with them. Involve children in missions conferences and prayer meetings. Have them participate in 'clean up days' at the church, taking responsibility for their place of worship. These brief suggestions provide only a start, and the limit is your creativity.

Parents, I don't want to forget you. If you are not members of a local congregation, you are isolating yourselves from the faith community and its blessings. You are thus depriving your children of the ministry it offers and thus hindering your very own children. If you are not a part of a local church, join one that honours God and ministers to your children. Don't just attend, but be a full part of the community.

For those parents who are active in churches, faithfully teach your children their value in God's sight and in that of the church. We are often inclined to speak ill of the church, but this can distort our children's perceptions of the truth of the matter.

I close with a wonderful quote from G. Campbell Morgan, a pastor who obviously made children a priority. It sums up this chapter better than I can.

> We can never help our own children, the children in our own home, the children in our schools, the children of the nation, until we have caught Christ's vision of God's Kingdom, and until that has become the master passion of our lives. The Church, spending its strength on disputes concerning doctrines, wasting its time in quarrelling about ecclesiastical formulae, becoming worldly and self-centred, always neglects the child. On the other hand, the church, seeking the Kingdom, restless in the midst of everything that is contrary to the will of God; passionately desiring the building of His

city, and the bringing in of His rule—that church always seeks the child. A vision of and desire for the Kingdom of God is the master passion in all work for the children.[9]

10

CHILDREN AND THE SACRAMENTS

'It is understandable that the Reformation should state emphatically that baptism had come in the place of circumcision, not in a sense that makes infant baptism unlawful, but as one of the strongest arguments for the lawfulness of infant baptism' (G. C. Berkouwer).

'A man ought to examine himself before he eats of the bread and drinks of the cup' (1 Cor. 11:28).

One of the great privileges of being in the church is participating in the sacraments that our Lord has given to us. These manifest his grace and strengthen us in the faith. Since we understand that children are part of the visible body of Christ, how do they relate to these sacred institutions? Prayerfully join me on an expedition into the intriguing realm of children and the sacraments.

Immersed in controversy and sprinkled with doubt: Children and Baptism

More ink, emotion, and even blood, has been spilled over the topic of infant baptism than on any other topic we have considered. The subject is notorious for spurring discussions that commonly produce more heat than light. This is primarily a modern controversy, for infant baptism was a 'given' for much of church history, though 'believers' baptism' has gained favour recently.

Why the debate? The answer is simple. The New Testament does not give us a definitive command, 'Thou shalt baptize infants,' nor its opposite, 'Thou shalt not baptize infants.' This means we must find our answer by approaching the limited specific information from the perspective of all of Scripture. However, many of the discussions of the issue flow from uninformed opinion or simplistic theology, leading to arguments that are more emotional than biblical.

Unlike many of the issues we have covered, a great deal has been written on the subject of infant baptism.[1] I will try to summarize the covenant tradition here as it follows from the perspective I have presented in the rest of this book. While such a discussion has potential to be divisive, a thorough understanding of children within the church requires us to address it.

Just the facts

Let us begin our discussion by summarizing what the New Testament says about baptism. First, Jesus ordains baptism in the Great Commission of Matthew 28:19–20. This establishes it as a sacrament. Second, Acts repeatedly shows that those making professions of faith during the early years of the church were baptized. In each case these were adults, cognitively capable of understanding what was happening. Third, the only biblical cases suggesting children were baptized were 'household baptisms' where all family members were baptized when the head made a profession of faith. We must assume that households included children, and Scripture nowhere states that each child baptized made a profession of faith. On the other hand, this is not stated specifically. The New Testament does not give an account of a child being saved or baptized, so we must derive our position from our understanding of Scripture as a whole. The approach we are taking is much like how we understand the Trinity. Though it is never explained directly in the Bible, the broad perspective of the Scripture shows it to be true.

A quick review

Let me set the stage for our discussion by reminding you of some of the relevant ideas we have already covered. Children are born in sin, having a sinful nature long before they knowingly commit particular sinful acts. They therefore are subject to the judgment of God, but can be saved by God's grace none the less. We also saw that Jesus took children brought to him by parents and blessed them even though they were not old enough to initiate this themselves. He even said that his kingdom is comprised of such children. In Chapter 9 we learned that children have a place of importance within the covenant. Their inclusion makes sense, for it would seem strange for God to give children as gifts then give believing parents no particular hope of their salvation. As part of God's people, these children were entitled to receive the sign of the covenant.

Circumcision: sign of the covenant

We saw in our last chapter that circumcision was essential to the covenant of grace that God made with Abraham. In a sense, the two are even to be equated. Genesis 17:10 declares, 'This is my covenant with you and your descendants after you, the covenant you are to keep: Every male among you shall be circumcised.' This correlation accounts for Stephen's use of the term, 'the covenant of circumcision' (Acts 7:8). It is therefore evident that circumcision was the sign of the covenant of grace in the Old Testament.

We will learn in our discussion of baptism that it carries a manifold significance, and so it was with circumcision. Our initial observation as to the meaning of circumcision is that in itself it carried no power, but served as 'a physical sign representing the spiritual meaning of the covenant'.[2] An 'exit' sign simply shows the way out of a place, but does not necessarily mean we actually leave. Similarly, circumcision pointed to God's promise but did not guarantee its spiritual benefits for those without faith. At the same time, as Jesus blessed the children, so circumcision and baptism are signs of his blessing.

Circumcision can be seen as signifying several different things, and we will list them without going into much detail. Observe as you review them that none of these things become obsolete with Christ, and are important for believers today just as they were when they were written. These include:

1. The seal of the covenant of grace as summarized in Leviticus 26:12, 'I will...be your God, and you will be my people.' This covenant showed that the Jews were saved by grace on the basis of faith, just as we are today (cp. Eph. 2:8–9).

2. Communion of God with his people, as seen in the same text, 'I will walk among you.'

3. The removal of defilement, exemplified by the texts (Deut. 10:16; Jer. 4:4; Ezek. 44:7) alluding to circumcision of the heart as purity.

4. Similarly, circumcision signified the righteousness of faith as Paul observed in Romans 4:11.

5. Calvin tells us of the significance of circumcision as representing repentance in references such as Jeremiah 4:4 and 9:25.[3] The phrase 'all who are circumcised only in the flesh' in the latter is noteworthy in how crisply it distinguished the external sign from the internal grace.

These, then, were the implications of circumcision for the Jewish infants who received it. These meanings held despite the recipients being mentally incapable of understanding them, and despite their sometimes not growing into the faith of Abraham.

The relationship of circumcision to baptism

This is a central point, for our argument thus far would mean that we would still need to circumcise infants given the continuity of the covenant. In Jesus' Great Commission (Matt. 28:19–20), baptism is declared to be the sign of the covenant for the church age. For, as circumcision was in the Old Testament church, 'baptism is the badge and symbol of entrance into the New Testament church.'[4] As such, it is to be applied as circumcision was in the Old.

The Scriptures help us reason this through better. Consider 1 Corinthians 7:14: 'For the unbelieving husband has been sanctified through his wife, and the unbelieving wife has been sanctified through her believing husband. Otherwise your children would be unclean, but as it is, they are holy.' Care must be taken to remember that 'holy' need not always mean totally pure, but means 'set apart'. In some sense, children of believers are set apart, and the nature of this can be inferred from the contrast with their being 'unclean'. Calvin thus notes that this text 'teaches that the children of the pious are set apart from others by a sort of exclusive privilege, so as to be reckoned holy in the Church', observing that this privilege 'flows from the blessing of the covenant.'[5] John Murray remarks that this holiness 'can be nothing less than the "holiness" of connection and privilege'[6] of the covenant.

Children of believers, then, are different from others by virtue of the covenant blessing just as was true in the Old Testament. This should not surprise us, for we would not expect children of Christian parents to be less favoured by God than children of the Jewish faithful. It is altogether appropriate that they should receive the sign of the covenant. But what should that sign be?

Those familiar with the debate over infant baptism may well be familiar with Colossians 2:11–12, which states, 'In him you were also circumcised, in the putting off of the sinful nature, not with a circumcision done by the hands of men but with the circumcision done by Christ, having been buried with him in baptism, and raised with him through your faith in the power of God, who raised him from the dead.' Here the apostle explains that the 'circumcision made without hands' is the same as 'having been buried with him in baptism'. Circumcision is replaced as the sign of the covenant by baptism, a rite without the shedding of blood since Jesus' blood has now been shed and no more is needed.

In sum, there is nothing in the New Testament to justify terminating the sign of God's covenant to children of believers, and baptism has replaced circumcision as that sign. Therefore, as Jesus welcomed children for his blessing when parents brought them to him, so we as faithful parents should not be shy to bring our children for the covenant blessing.

The significance of baptism

Logic would suggest that we take a moment to establish the meaning of baptism in general so that we might see how that can be applied to infants. There are numerous truths represented in baptism; it is a profoundly 'deep' symbol of the truth it is designed to reflect. We will briefly cover some of the major meanings of baptism after a note on what is meant by a 'sign.'

We observed earlier that a 'sign' is not the same as that to which it points. Though baptism signifies God's grace, it is not the same as that grace. Murray writes, 'Baptism does not convey or confer the grace which it signifies.'[7] In a complimentary manner, Calvin observes that baptism signifies regeneration but does not communicate it.[8] Physical baptism does not bestow the blessings it symbolizes, and this is a critical point to bear in mind in the following discussion, for recipients of baptism receive the symbol independent of the grace it represents, though in response to the promises of that grace.

Let us review some of the major meanings associated with the sacrament of baptism. The order they are presented in will allow comparison with the meanings of circumcision listed above.

SIGN OF THE COVENANT PROMISES

We have alluded to some of the reasoning for this already, and Neilands states the heart of the matter, 'We demonstrate our faith in God's covenant promises when in obedience to God's commandment we bring our children for baptism. By faith we claim these promises for our covenant children.'[9] Hereby is baptism seen as the New Testament sign of the covenant, comparable to circumcision in the Old, and administered in like manner (though with the obvious exception that girls, too, receive the New Testament sign).

SIGN OF MEMBERSHIP IN THE CHURCH

This would lead to the benefits of God's communion with his people as we noted in the second meaning of circumcision. Proponents of infant baptism, like many of their brethren, make a distinction between members of the visible and invisible churches, the latter constituting the truly elect, the former those who are merely associated with the church. *The Westminster Confession* defines the visible church to consist of 'all those throughout the world that profess the true religion, together with their children'.[10] Noah's family was spared because of his faith. Abraham's offspring were included with him in God's blessing. In the New Testament, new converts were joined in baptism by their families. Even so, children of believing parents are counted as part of the church. This is to the advantage of the child. Calvin observes, 'The children receive some benefit from their baptism: being engrafted into the body of the church, they are somewhat more commended to the other members. Then, when they have grown up, they are greatly spurred to an earnest zeal for worshiping God.'[11] This agrees with Paul who addressed children as being among the churches receiving his epistles (e.g. Eph. 6:1 and Col. 3:20). Even G. R. Beasley-Murray, writing in a Baptist publication, recognizes (commenting on 1 Cor. 7:14), that 'Paul suggests that it is possible to come within the sphere of the church's blessing without actually being a confessed member.'[12]

FORGIVENESS OF SIN

This is simply another way of stating that baptism signifies the removal of defilement (see, for example, Acts 2:38). The baptism of a person reflects a cleansing from the impurity of sin, this being the obvious symbolism of the application of water. As with circumcision, of course, true 'baptism' is of the heart, and those who are pure of heart seek God and obey him. This purity is not caused by the sacrament, but is the truth that baptism is designed to reflect, just as was the case with circumcision as described above. External baptism alone purifies the recipient no more than circumcision did, but signifies the inward working of the Spirit of God.

REPENTANCE AND FAITH

'Repent...and be baptized' are the words of the apostle Peter in Acts 2:38. Those who baptize infants agree that adults should repent before being baptized, but what of children?

Circumcision looked to a turning from sin (repentance) in the life of the child on whom it was performed. For the maturing child, this would have been seen in an inclination to obedience to God and not necessarily to a life of rebellion with a sudden conversion to following God. The child Samuel (1 Sam. 1–3) exemplifies this well, being literally called by God from childhood with no period of blatantly sinful living from which to turn. The turn was from the sinful direction of his fallen nature, with him apparently being regenerated from infancy (as with Jeremiah, Jer. 1:5).

Faith is involved, but not simply that of the person receiving it. The body of Christ hopes in the promise of God that the child being baptized has an 'infant faith' and that this will grow into a personally professed faith. But parents also demonstrate faith similar to that of the parents who brought their little ones to Jesus for his gracious blessing without those children having professed their faith themselves. Most specifically, the child's parents and the church community express faith in the covenant of God when the sacrament of baptism is administered. We must believe in God's promises and power to forgive sin and grant new life. For those holding to infant baptism, this faith is rooted in the covenant promise of God. Those who insist that the basis for baptizing someone is their profession of faith alone are forced to trust largely in that individual's word, a precarious undertaking at best. Surely the greater confidence is to be placed in the promise of our Holy God.

REGENERATION

Few argue against the idea that baptism is a sign of new birth. We are born spiritually dead because of original sin, and baptism is a sign of our new life. Infants, as we saw in Chapter 4, cannot be excluded from the realm of God's regenerating grace. If the covenant means that believers have a particular hope that their children will come to faith, there is reason to administer the sign of this hope to these covenant children. In the past, regeneration was often seen as a process, not a sudden conversion. So, Calvin queries, 'I ask, what the danger is if infants be said to receive now some part of that grace which in a little while they shall enjoy to the full?'[13] Calvin believed that regeneration could have roots in infancy, but this still means the child must eventually show signs of being born again.

My hope has been to show that each meaning attributed to the sign of baptism has parallels in circumcision, and that there is adequate justification for applying it to children. Though baptism will always carry some sense of mystery and wonder, there is much encouragement in realizing the rich beauty of its meaning, and in knowing that our children are to share in it.

The New Testament rationale for infant baptism

We now see that there are important similarities in the meaning of circumcision and baptism. We have already commented on the lack of a definitive New Testament command on the subject of infant baptism, so we need to demonstrate how these two practices fulfil the same purpose. In developing the doctrine from this portion of God's Word, we would be prudent to keep in mind that because the context of early Christianity was largely Jewish, they would have been well-versed in the revelation God had given to Israel and thus inclined to place their theology in that context. As a result, they would be inclined to affirm with Murray that 'A commandment of Scripture is binding until its obligation ceases, or it is repealed, or it is modified.'[14] So the greater burden is to show that there is now no covenant sign for the children of believers. There is no word of repeal in the New Testament, and logically it would seem a step backward for God to provide a covenant sign for his people in the Old Testament but not today.

One problem in developing the New Testament practice of baptism is that the text covers only the initial expansion period of the church, and thus says little or nothing about second-generation Christians. The only verse on this next generation that comes to mind is 2 Timothy 1:5 where Paul comments about Timothy, 'I have been reminded of your sincere faith, which first lived in your grandmother Lois and in your mother Eunice and, I am persuaded, now lives in you also.' If anything, this argues for the covenant view of faith being passed on primarily within the family context. Notice that Paul saw Timothy's faith as having first lived in his grandmother and mother, though admittedly this says nothing of Timothy's baptism.

In Acts 2:39 Peter makes clear that the promise still includes children. This is put into practice in Acts 16:14–15 when Lydia responds to the gospel and is baptized with 'her household'. The same pattern holds true in the conversion of the Philippian jailer later in the same chapter (vv. 31–3), where Paul and Silas specifically say that by the jailer's faith he and his household will be saved, and upon his profession he was baptized along with his household. Paul recalls baptizing 'the household of Stephanas' in 1 Corinthians 1:16, and Acts 11:14 mentions the salvation of another that included his household. There is therefore a definite pattern whereby the entire household is baptized when an adult in the family makes a profession of faith.

There are two possible explanations for these household baptisms: (1) All of the members of every one of these households were of age and immediately made their own decision for Christ when they saw their parent doing so. We must in this view assume there were no infants or young children in any of these cases; (2) Given the context of Peter's inclusion of children, these household baptisms reflect the application of this principle as young and old children were included, as would be expected when several different households are mentioned.

The latter option is by far the more reasonable. Luke and Paul would have done well to specify 'adult members of the household' if they intended to exclude an entire age-group that the Greek does not call for. Thus, while infants are not specifically mentioned in these verses, it appears probable that they were included in the households mentioned. Couple this with Jesus' command in Matthew 19:14 to 'Let the little children come to me, and do not hinder them,' and one is hard pressed to find a biblical rationale for leaving infants and young children entirely out of the picture of New Testament baptism.

To summarize, it appears that baptism replaces circumcision as the sign of the covenant to God's people today. While, like circumcision, it is to be applied to adults who come to faith, it is also to be administered to the children of those in the believing community as a sign of faith in the covenant and hope for the salvation of these covenant children. Since it is a sign, it does not in itself impart grace, but represents the grace that inheres in the promise of God. It also shows that our children are a part of the community of faith which is the church, and thereby entitled to the blessings and nurturance found there.

Whose children are to be baptized?

The promises of the covenant are to Abraham and his offspring of faith. It follows directly that those who are not of faith are not of the promise and their children should not receive its sign. In other words, those who do not profess faith in God should not be permitted to bring their children for baptism today. Murray explains:

> Only those united to Christ in the virtue of his death and in the efficacy and power of his resurrection have the right before God to claim the promises of the covenant of grace; only such can claim the privilege which God bestows upon their children and the promises He gives in respect of them to His covenant people.[15]

If parents who confess faith in Christ and live a life suggestive of regeneration present their children for baptism, it should be offered. One's own baptism as an infant is not sufficient to permit bringing one's children, for we have learned that baptism does not automatically demonstrate the genuineness of one's faith. Those baptized in infancy who rebel against the covenant promises and live ungodly lives forfeit the privileges of the covenant, including the right to have their children baptized. History shows the failure of experiments to baptize the children of those outside the visible church. However, in our day it is not likely that those outside the church would seek baptism for their children.

The beauty of baptizing infants

We live in a threatening world. Christians increasingly are being pushed to the 'fringes' of modern society as it strains its every muscle to pull our children away from us into its grip of death. Were there no promise of God, no particular hope for our children in the midst of a pagan culture, we would be inclined to question God's telling us that children are gifts. What pain they can cause when they stray, and what sorrow for parents when they consider the world into which they are commanded to bring children by being fruitful and multiplying. If there is no promise, we are a people to be pitied.

But, God be praised, this is not the case. We have cause to hope for our children, the cause being the promise of God. He has ordained to build his church largely from her offspring, and has given us comfort in his promise. How can we deny marking our children as God's in infancy? This places them under the wing of the Almighty and the prospects for a blessed life and afterlife. Though they may not at the time experience the joy, baptism is not designed to be a memorable 'experience'. Children of believers are to grow in the awareness that God has staked a claim on their lives and provided for and protected them. This is the joy for the growing child as she or he comes to understand the beauty of having been baptized.

Parents, too, find much comfort in God's promise. This is fitly summarized by John Calvin who demonstrates his pastor's heart by exhorting, 'Let us accept as incontrovertible that God is so good and generous to his own as to be pleased, for their sake, also to count among his people the children whom they have begotten.'[16] Let us not deny them the sign of God's covenant, or ourselves the comfort of knowing and proclaiming that our children are under God's blessing.

Children at the table of the Lord

I confess I experience some mild anxiety on Sundays when we observe communion at our church. I consider it an honour to partake of the sacrament and seek to do so in humility. However, these days we can predict being asked by our eight-year-old daughter, 'Why can't I take it with you?' Though we have had the discussion a number of times, she still doesn't quite grasp it. Most of us think that young children shouldn't take communion, but we may not understand why. It took a child to motivate me to study this and think it through. Children, after all, often notice things we overlook. Let me share with you what I've learned.

THE DEVELOPMENT OF THE PASSOVER MEAL

You will recall that this ceremony has its origin in the deliverance of the Israelites from Egyptian bondage under Moses. The inaugural directions are given to Moses and Aaron in Exodus 12:1–13. The context was that this would be a testimony to the angel of the Lord as it passed over Egypt so that the firstborn of each household would be spared. It then follows naturally that this was observed household by household, blood from the family lamb being spread on the doorposts with the flesh being eaten by the family. Reminiscent of the household baptisms described earlier, the biblical language does not specify whether young children were to eat, but certainly the implication was there.

The location for the Passover was centralized according to Deuteronomy 16:1–8. The Hebrew families would gather together for this commemorative celebration. It served to remind them not only of their deliverance from Egypt, but of the necessity of the shedding of blood for their deliverance from their sins.

JESUS AND THE PASSOVER

Jesus not only celebrated Passover, he actually became our Passover. As Paul clearly stated, 'Christ, our Passover lamb, has been sacrificed' (1 Cor. 5:7). Here is weighty evidence that the apostle saw the Passover as a prefiguring of the death of Jesus and thus ties these two events together closely and provides reasonable grounds for seeing the Lord's Supper as related to the Passover. Other places in Scripture refer to Jesus as the Lamb of God (e.g. John 1:29 and frequently in Revelation).

Paul's comments reflect Jesus' actual use of his last Passover meal to show himself to be the Passover Lamb, and that the disciples were to partake of him. The accounts of the Last Supper are found in Matthew 26:26–35, Mark 14:22–31 and Luke 22:14–23. (John 13–17 gives the greatest detail of Jesus' teaching that night, but curiously omits the institution of the Lord's Supper.) Jesus changed the 'menu' for the meal significantly. No longer would it include the shedding of blood, for his blood was to be shed shortly and there would be no more need for animal sacrifices. Even as the bloodshed of circumcision is eliminated in baptism, so the animal blood of Passover is replaced with the wine in the Lord's Supper, symbolizing Jesus' blood shed for our sins. The bread, of course, comes to stand for his body given for us, the substance of our eternal life (John 6:48–51). The Passover's connection to the Lord's Supper serves to show this as a continuous sign for God's people, reflecting the provision for their sins and salvation.

COMMANDS REGARDING PARTAKING OF THE SUPPER

However, the New Testament outlines additional commands regarding the Lord's Supper. Unlike baptism, the recipient of the bread and wine is not passive, he is active, engaging in a behaviour rather than passively receiving a sign. This active role of the recipient may underlie the conditions that Scripture attaches to coming to the table in a proper manner, and explain our caution in bringing our children to the table.

'Do this in remembrance of me' (Luke 22:19). Here our Lord makes a direct command to his disciples that memory is a part of coming to the table. Communion is an act (suggesting positive action) of remembering, and thus to obey our Lord's commands we must recall the work of Christ as we partake of the supper of Christ. Thus it is that the words of Jesus are repeated when the supper is given, aiding the memory of those who are participating.

'For whenever you eat this bread and drink this cup, you proclaim the Lord's death until he comes' (1 Cor. 11:26). One must understand in order to confess, and that this understanding is a prerequisite is made clear by the ensuing verses that warn of judgment to those who wrongly partake of the Supper. As Calvin states, 'If...you would celebrate the Supper aright, you must bear in mind, that a profession of faith is required of you.'[17]

'A man ought to examine himself' (1 Cor. 11:28). The apostle now instructs us to put ourselves to the test before coming to the supper lest we profane the table, and thus bring weakness, sickness, or even death upon us (v. 30). There is no doubt that Paul is quite sincere in his admonition here: to partake of the supper wrongfully is serious business, and to err is to provoke divine wrath. No such qualifications are placed on circumcision, baptism, or the Passover. Calvin summarizes the faith which is proper for the table, 'If . . . thou aspirest after the righteousness of God with the earnest desire of thy mind, and, humbled under a view of thy misery, dost wholly lean upon Christ's grace, and rest upon it, know that thou art a worthy guest to approach that table.'[18]

Such examination requires a considerable degree of reason and power of reflection, things obviously lacking in young children. To permit such to the Lord's Supper is to ignore the applicability of Paul's warning, a daring move given the terrifying consequences that might follow. It is thus advised that, for their protection, children should be denied the Supper until they reach a point where they can reflect upon their faith.

'Anyone who eats and drinks without recognizing the body...' (1 Cor. 11:29). This condition directly follows the former. One of the matters about which we are to examine ourselves is whether we can judge the body rightly, which means how well we can discern the spiritual nature of the meal. To protect our children, we need to deny them the Table until we are confident they understand its significance.

It is apparent that young children cannot fulfil these commands, and risk spiritual harm if they partake of the Lord's Supper before they can. This is the logic behind the denial of access to the Table for young children. But how might we know when our children are ready? We will answer that in Chapter 12.

So, to answer my daughter's question, I respond in kind, 'Do you really understand why we do this?' When she replies in the negative, I proceed to explain that as she grows and understands more of the faith, and continues to learn to love and obey God, she will have opportunity to share in the Supper. The present exclusion, for her protection, serves to encourage her to grow in her faith. Meanwhile, we will continue instructing her in the things of the Lord and keep her active in our community of faith. We pray God will continue his work in her life and make her truly his. We expectantly await the day when she will join us in communion.

11

FROM THE MOUTHS OF BABES

Children and Worship

'A certain little child, when he could not speak plainly, would
be crying after God, and was greatly desirous to be taught
good things. He could not endure to be put to bed without
family prayer, but would put his parents upon duty and would
with much devotion kneel down and with great patience
and delight continue till duty was at an end without the least
expression of being weary. And he seemed never so well-
pleased as when he was engaged in prayer. He could not be
satisfied with family prayer but would often be upon his knees
by himself in one corner or another. He was much delighted
to hear the Word of God either preached or read' (James
Janeway, A *Token for Children*).

You may have guessed that the true story told above is not
a contemporary one. It is rare enough to hear of family prayer,
but even more unusual to modern ears is the thought of a child so
eager to pray and hear the Bible read. Because we rarely see this,
we may be inclined to think it is impossible. Some theologians
would say it is impossible for children to worship God because

they cannot be saved until they are old enough to make a rational profession of faith, and thus are unfit to worship God. The scriptural story is quite different, and the infrequency of children's worship today may reflect more on our attitudes than on our children. The purpose of this chapter is to demonstrate that the Bible is straightforward in affirming children in worshipping the Almighty, and to raise awareness of steps we might take to have glory brought to God through the participation of our children in worship.

Biblical references to children worshipping

A beautiful strand of references runs through God's Word declaring the praise of children and infants. Let's begin with the Psalms. Psalm 8:2 says, 'From the lips of children and infants you have ordained praise.' Spurgeon invites us to see 'how clearly the history of the church expounds this verse',[1] referring to the frequent testimony of praise from the lips of children. In Psalm 148 the entire creation is exhorted to praise, including (v. 12) 'young men and maidens, old men and children'. Here again it is evident that children are to join in the worshipful chorus of praise to God.

In Matthew 21:15–16 the Pharisees become indignant when children in the temple cry out, 'Hosanna to the Son of David' (v. 15). Note first that children were in the temple, a place of worship, to begin with. Then observe how Jesus takes this opportunity to 'exegete' Psalm 8:2 for us, applying it to how these little children recognized the Son of David when the learned, self-righteous chief priests and scribes failed to discern who Jesus was. Calvin explains, 'Since the praises of God are heard from the tongue of infants [in Jesus' reference to Psalm 8:2], Christ infers from this, that it is not strange if He cause them to be uttered by children who have already acquired the use of speech.'[2] Jesus rebukes the religious leaders, not the children. This passage shows that Jesus gladly received the praise of children.

Several other passages less clearly refer to young children worshipping. Ecclesiastes 12:1 encourages early piety, exhorting 'Remember your Creator in the days of your youth, before the days of trouble come and the years approach when you will say, "I find no pleasure in them.'" This text appears to point to the value of meditation on God in one's youth as an inoculation against later disinterest in the things of God. Psalm 71:5 reads, 'For you have been my hope, O Sovereign LORD, my confidence since my youth.' This is not a direct reference to worship, but demonstrates that the psalmist took comfort in God from his early years.

If children can offer worship that pleases God, how were they involved in the formal worship described in Scripture?

Children in the formal worship of the Old Testament

The Old Testament gives us indication that children were present at formal worship 'services' as part of the covenant community. Let us consider some passages describing this.

Exodus 12:24 and 26–7 highlight aspects of the Passover and Feast of Unleavened Bread. This ordinance was established 'for you and your descendants' (v. 24), specifically including children in the event as seen in our last chapter. Part of the purpose for their inclusion was to arouse their curiosity, and bring them to ask, 'What does this ceremony mean?' (v. 26). Participation in the festival, whether active or not, led to questions about worship and thus encouraged and improved worship.

Deuteronomy 29:10–13 and 31:10–13 describe assemblies of the people of God that explicitly included children. The former describes the covenant in Moab where 'children' (v. 11; 'little ones' in the New American Standard Version) are part of the list of those who enter into the covenant. Richard Bacon observes that the Hebrew translated 'children' or 'little ones' means 'toddlers',[3] suggesting that children of two or three years were participants. The latter passage contains Moses' counsel for the future. The Law is to be read publicly every seven years as part of the Feast of Booths, partly because children 'who do not know this law, must hear it and learn to fear the LORD your God' (v. 13). This again shows that one purpose for including children in corporate worship is for instruction. Interestingly, if this ceremony were held every seven years, those who were hearing it for the first time would be those born since the last assembly. This would include those children under seven years of age. Joshua was faithful to keep this command (Josh. 8:35) where again 'little ones' are explicitly included among those who heard him read the Law to the people. Where are the children of this age in our churches when the Word is proclaimed?

We read in 2 Chronicles 20 of the threat made to Judah by an alliance of enemy kings. Jehoshaphat calls for fasting and a prayer meeting. Was this just for adults? No, for this was serious business that impacted all of the people of God. The text goes out of its way to inform us that no age was overlooked. Two different words are used in verse 13 to describe children among the participants, 'And all the men of Judah, with their wives and children and little ones, stood there before the LORD.' Children were a part of this vital prayer meeting and were apparently even called upon to fast.

Celebration was the order of the day when, under Nehemiah's leadership, the wall of Jerusalem was completed. In Nehemiah 12:43, we read that '...on that day they offered great sacrifices, rejoicing because God had given them great joy. The women and children also rejoiced.' These children rejoiced because they were a vital part of this worshipping community, as they should be today as well.

In Joel 2:15–16 God's prophet exhorts the people to declare a holy fast and to gather in a sacred assembly. He specifically includes 'children' and 'those nursing at the breast' (v. 16) among the invited, declaring them to be a part of the sacred assembly as well.

In surveying this history of the Old Testament, and as we recollect that families were the unit of God's working in the New Testament when adults were converted, we see that children are considered by God as part of his covenant community. Richard Bacon consequently observes, 'There is not a single Scripture passage indicating that children should routinely be excluded from the regular worship services of the church.[4]

Specific examples of children worshipping

We have reviewed the commands and practices of including children in corporate worship in the Old Testament. We turn now to look at some examples of individuals who worshipped God during their tender years. We will not include David here as his recollections were noted when we looked at the Psalms earlier.

In accordance with Deuteronomy 12:17–18, Elkanah's family is portrayed as sharing in his sacrifice. 1 Samuel 1:4 relates that 'whenever the day came for Elkanah to sacrifice, he would give portions of the meat to his wife Peninnah and to all her sons and daughters'. Again we see the family emphasis of worship.

This is, of course, merely the introduction to the far more familiar story of Elkanah's other wife, Hannah, and her long-awaited son, Samuel. As the story proceeds through the first chapter of 1 Samuel, God grants Hannah this son, and she gives him to the Lord (quite literally, leaving him at the house of the Lord). The text indicates that at this point Samuel, who had just been weaned, 'worshipped the LORD' (v. 28). This means that he could have realistically been no more than three years of age when genuine worship is attributed to him. Later, young Samuel (2:18) 'was ministering before the Lord—a boy wearing a linen ephod'. We lose track of his exact age, but his being quite young is evident in his mother's making him a 'little robe' (v. 19) from year to year. Samuel was still described as a 'boy' in 1 Samuel 3 when we read of his continuing to minister before the Lord and receiving a direct call from God. Thus Samuel is a powerful example of how our Lord can work in the life of a child, and how very young children can serve and worship God.

Our next instance of the faith and worship of a child is the young king Josiah. We read in 2 Kings 22:1–2 and 2 Chronicles 34:1–3 that Josiah began his reign at eight years of age and that he 'did what was right in the eyes of the LORD.' The Chronicles account adds that in the eighth year of his reign he 'began to seek the God of his father David' (v. 3). Young piety is seen in this king, and worship was certainly a part of this. Josiah went on to have a desire to please God throughout his career.

Consider the contrast with another young king. Jehoash became king over Judah at the tender age of seven (2 Kings 11:21), and began his career well by doing right in the sight of the Lord (2 Kings 12:2). Unlike Josiah, he strayed from the apparent faith of his early years. This serves as a warning not to take signs of piety for granted and to continue to nurture the spiritual lives of our children, praying that they remain faithful to our Lord.

In the New Testament we see Jesus in the temple at the age of 12 (Luke 2:41–50), and recall the spiritual joy that moved John the Baptist even in the womb (Luke 1:41). Paul reminds Timothy in 2 Timothy 3:15 how from 'infancy' he had known the holy Scriptures. Spirituality is not reserved for adults, and we see in these examples praise from John, worship from Jesus, and scriptural training for Timothy.

To summarize, our review of God's Word shows that he is glorified by the worship of children. He commands their inclusion in the worship of his people, and was careful to include numerous examples of child worship in Scripture. Aspects mentioned include hearing the proclamation of the Word, praying, singing, serving, and even fasting. Children were thus welcome at corporate worship in addition to family and private worship. The family of God today should endeavour to be as inclusive of children as our fathers and mothers of old. We would not deprive our children of the extraordinary privilege of participating in the worship of our holy God.

Applying what we have learned

If we stop to contemplate what we have discussed thus far, our hearts have cause to rejoice in the goodness and power of God who ordains praise from the mouths of babes, and acts in such a way as to make it possible. Yet, we cannot miss the central role we as parents and spiritual leaders are to play, even sensing some fear lest we fail to heed our Lord's command not to hinder children from coming to him. We would do well to think through some of the implications of the worship of children.

INCLUSION IN PUBLIC WORSHIP

Children hold a place of importance in the covenant community, which is the church. They were specifically involved in the worship of the faith community in the Old Testament. While the New Testament does not speak much of children in the worship of the assembly, their being addressed by Paul in his letters suggests that they were included in worship in New Testament times. How does this compare with modern church practices regarding children?

As we observed in Chapter 9, churches today vary in how they include children in their worship. They may have a children's sermon during the service, or possibly the children may be excused from the preaching to go to a separate 'junior church'. Our youngest ones are likely to be cared for in crêches or nurseries, ostensibly to free parents to worship and to minimize distractions in the services. Should we keep infants away from worship? Should we customize the experiences of older children, yet in so doing separate them from the worship of the faith community?

Richard Bacon argues strongly for the complete elimination of separate children's activities during worship,[5] believing that all children should be with their families in the service. He insists that faithfulness to the teaching of the Bible (where children are included with the entire body) is of more importance than any negative impact children might have on the solemn atmosphere of worship. He proposes the use of 'crier rooms' instead, areas adjacent to the sanctuary where the service can be viewed through a partition by parents who retreat there when their children become disruptive. A loud-speaker allows for the service to be heard, and the intention is that those in this room are part of the service, the room not being used for idle talk among those there.

This is a fairly absolute position, but many churches would do well to move in this direction. Often children in crêches or nurseries are offered no spiritual instruction or worship opportunity at all. However, given what we saw with three-year-old Samuel, we may need to reconsider our low expectations of young children.

Many churches have developed 'junior church' programmes where children too old for a crêche but deemed too young to sit quietly through the worship service are separated from the congregation to have a service of their own. The spirit of this is commendable, but the consequences of such need to be considered. First, there is no biblical precedent for such, and indeed this goes contrary to the many instances we have seen where children were specifically included in worship. For the sake of 'age-appropriate' instruction, children are separated from their families and removed from the preaching of the Word. This compromises the parents' opportunity to discuss the sermon with their families after church, specifically helping younger children to learn from the passage that was taught. Can we assume that they cannot worship or be blessed simply because they lack the cognitive skills we have? Scripture says we cannot, and should not, assume this. This is not to mention the instructional value of the worship time. Recall my daughter's questions about the Lord's Supper. Observing the elements of worship in the service is a powerful way to learn of our God and his proper worship. Discussion of the service afterward affords a blessed time of family interaction.

Please do not understand me to be saying that I do not think churches should have age-graded programmes. I believe this is important in Christian education programmes. However, the benefits of worshipping God as a family are great, and it seems unwise to deprive families of this opportunity.

THE VALUE OF THE WORSHIP OF CHILDREN

Many would assert that children cannot praise God or worship him at all until they have come of age and made a rational profession of faith. While we applaud the zeal of these persons to protect God against any hint of false worship, we must reject their position because of the dramatic import of Scripture to the contrary. All indications are that God not only can be praised by children, but that he wants to be, and warns us about standing in the way of their worship. If we must risk error in some way, it seems far better to risk some of their praise being insincere than to cut them off from the opportunity. I imagine children are not the only ones in most churches who offer insincere worship at times.

I would also remind you of the privilege of family worship. This is explicitly designed to be inclusive of all ages while allowing more accommodations for the younger participants. You might choose to review the guidelines I offered at the end of chapter 5.

We have seen that children were an integral part of the corporate worship of the faith community of old. God also values their worship. Let us, then, consider how we might enhance the offerings of worship our children can bring before God's throne.

I find the whole notion of children praising our Lord exhilarating. It prompts me to worship the One whom, though Almighty, exults in being praised by the weakest members of our families. This spirit is found in a hymn attributed to Clement of Alexandria (c. AD 200).[6]

> Shepherd of tender youth,
> Guiding in love and truth
> Through devious ways:
> Christ, our triumphant King,
> We come thy Name to sing;
> Hither our children bring,
> To shout thy praise.
> So now and till we die,
> Sound we thy praises high,
> And joyful sing:
> Infants, and the glad throng
> Who to thy church belong,
> Unite to swell the song
> To Christ our King.

12

THE SPIRITUAL NURTURE
OF CHILDREN IN THE CHURCH

'*Feed my lambs*' (Jesus in John 21:15).

'*When I think of those who have influenced my life the most,
I think not of the great but of the good*' (John Knox).

She reminded me of the 'cute little red-haired girl' for whom
Charlie Brown had a crush in the 'Peanuts' comic strip. I had
been working with this seven-year-old for some weeks when
I happened to see her on the same day she had been to her
paediatrician. Curious about how she perceived my job, I asked,
'I don't have a white coat or a nurse, and I don't give medicine. So
what kind of doctor am I?' She thought a moment, and then gave
me the job description I use till this day, 'You're a doctor who
takes people who aren't sick and makes them better.'

I don't want to imply that our churches are sick, but from what
we have learned in the past three chapters, I would like to propose
some ways we might make them better. You may be a church
leader who can take some immediate steps, or a concerned parent
who is eager to make your church a richer source of spiritual

nurture for your child. Whoever you may be, please reflect on these suggestions prayerfully.

Prayer for our children

Let us begin with the most obvious. We observed at the outset of our journey that these are challenging times for our offspring as cultural forces vie for the lives of our children. As Christians, we recognize that there are spiritual forces behind these. But we also know 'The prayer of a righteous man is powerful and effective' (James 5:16b). Nothing is more basic to the fight for our children that a fervent appeal to the Almighty on their behalf.

I assume parents pray for their children and pastors pray for their flocks. My appeal is that our churches unite in more systematic and specific prayer for our little ones. I am eager to hear more prayer for our covenant children from our pulpits. I encourage churches to assign pastors, elders, or deacons to each family who will lift up each child in the family by name on at least a weekly basis. Churches could call occasional prayer-meetings for the stated purpose of praying for their children and youth. Leadership might set aside a weekly time for people to meet at the church to pray for their children. Men's and women's groups could have a marvellous ministry by praying for the youth of the church. Parents can meet informally to pray for each other's children. Sunday-school classes and other groups should consider adopting pregnant couples and praying for their unborn children. A couple might specifically be assigned to pray for each infant baptized in the church. Be creative with other ways to keep the church's children before the throne of grace.

The specificity of our prayer is central. Ask protection for our covenant children from the evils of our day, asking God to protect them from materialism, sexual sin and worldly thinking. Pray that he will guard their hearts from the negative influences that are unavoidable in our time. Pray positively for the children of your church to come to faith and to manifest the fruit of the Spirit, to obey the Ten Commandments, and to exhibit the other spiritual attitudes taught in Scripture. Pray for their education, their interests, their peer and dating relationships, and their safety. Seek God on behalf of parents, teachers, and others who minister to these little ones. God will show you numerous other areas that you can include in your supplications on behalf of the children. Offer all these prayers in thanksgiving for the divine gifts that our children are.

Mentors for children

Children learn much from relationships, the ones with their parents obviously being the most influential. When children have regular access to grandparents who love the Lord, they have further opportunity to see what faith looks like after it has matured even more. But rarely do children have close friendships with adults who are not related to them. Offering such a relationship could serve the cause of spiritual nurture quite well.

One way this might be done is for the church to assign a more mature couple to mentor families. They could give parents direction in child-rearing, offer prayer support, and befriend the children. The context for this could be sharing a meal and fellowship together on a regular basis, say every other week.

As children become adolescents, they often are more impressed by those who are only a few steps ahead of them on the road of life. Pairing junior or senior high-school students with college-aged young people who are strong in the faith could provide positive role-models to counter the ones these teens find in the popular media. This might just give them a 'taste' of the joy of living for Christ and the resource faith provides to these mentors as they deal with their problems.

My vision would be for each family and child of the church to have a mentor. That is unlikely, as this is admittedly a lofty goal. There may be a limited supply of people who show the maturity this would require. Conversely, it is unlikely that every family would want to participate anyway. Still, I urge you to seek our Lord's face as to whether he might have your church provide such a ministry.

Christian education

I can't ever recall being in a church that made no effort to educate their people in the faith. Nor have I visited a church that did not view including children in this programme as essential. My concern is not that we lack Christian education programmes for our children, but how well they serve the purpose in this day when so many negative influences pound at the doors of our children's hearts.

Sunday school is the cornerstone of most churches' educational programmes. Given the responsibilities and challenges parents face in nurturing children to follow Christ, we might offer classes for them. More mature parents could instruct the younger in effective Christian discipline and nurture. This would include, as we have seen, more than behaviour management. It would encompass the broad task of raising children to faith and service to God, including developing the Christian character of parents as they model godliness to their children. Small group studies are also appropriate for this type of training.

For the children themselves, we seem to do a good job of teaching them Bible stories. We appear less successful, as children mature, in teaching them the doctrines of the faith and a comprehensive worldview. The teaching of catechisms should prove helpful, especially if these were coordinated with efforts by the parents to do the same at home. In the past, this was a central task for pastors. As children became teenagers, these truths could be discussed in relation to the philosophies behind the popular music and media that are so tempting. Our saying 'no' to popular influences will be ineffective until our youth better understand why these influences are wrong. This understanding will come only when they see how their faith affects all areas of their thinking and their life.

An important aspect of this is teaching young people critical thinking (as we noted in chapter 6). Our educational programmes need to provide opportunity for teaching and practising these skills. For example, recent Disney movies have had a large measure of 'spirituality' in them, mostly new-age types of ideas. We cannot let our children be exposed to these uncritically. We need to teach them why we disapprove, whether we permit them to see the movies or not. A case in point is *The Little Mermaid*. In Disney's version, the teenage mermaid is frustrated by an irritable father and thus is justified in making a pact with a witch (standing in for the devil himself). This blatant act of rebellion and drawing upon the forces of evil convinces her father of his errant ways, leading to his backing off his principles and giving in to his daughter. We cannot let our children absorb such ideas without pointing them out and refuting them.

Though we should focus such training in critical thinking on our children and young people, we also need to provide a setting where such thinking can be taught to parents as well. Many parents are easily distracted from the dangers of the media because of the 'cuteness' with which it is portrayed.

Finally, churches can serve their families by helping them with academic choices. Scholarships to Christian schools could be budgeted, and more church schools founded. Resources might be made available to home-schoolers, including academic, spiritual and financial support. For example, our church has begun having a home-school study hall during its daytime women's meetings. This allows home-school mums to attend while the children can still do their schoolwork.

When should children take communion?

A major issue in the life of the church is when to accept the faith of children as genuine and admit them to full membership in the body. This includes the right to communion and the privilege of voting for church officers (in many churches).

We have seen that covenant children may gradually grow into faith, and may not experience a sudden conversion. How, then, may we know when they truly accept the faith for themselves? Can we determine a chronological age by which a child has matured to where he or she understands and intelligently assents to the Christian faith and is able to examine himself adequately enough to partake of the Lord's Supper?

Jewish boys have their Bar-Mitzvahs at thirteen. Fourteen has often been considered a minimum age for marriage in history, so puberty might serve as a guideline. Calvin suggested a lower age of about ten,[1] but had rather high expectations of achievement for that age.

Developmental psychology teaches us that children mature at different rates, though trends show they generally can tell the basics of right and wrong by the age of five or six, and develop the capacity for abstract reasoning by early adolescence. Though we might set a general guideline as somewhere between these two mile posts (putting us in the neighbourhood of Calvin's suggestion of ten), wisdom tells us that criteria other than age would be preferable for determining admission to the Lord's Table. After all, we are to judge their ability to understand Christ's work, and that will vary with age. We also need to determine whether their lives show evidence of their truly following Christ.

SUGGESTED CRITERIA

Criteria are widely used in our society for admission to certain privileges. For example, if I wish to practise medicine, I know I must go through a certain curriculum, obtain specific experience, and pass the appropriate examinations. This done successfully, I receive my licence to practise until I misuse it to the point of having it revoked.

Such a model of criteria could be used for admitting our children to full fellowship in the church and to the Lord's Table. This would also set a direction for parents in the training of their children, and for church education programmes as well. Once a child's parents and teachers believe the child professes a genuine faith and has mastered the specified criteria, the leaders of the church would examine that child. Upon verification of the child's testimony and character, he or she would be presented to the church as a form of public confession, and admitted to the Lord's Supper and membership in the body.

It is readily apparent that the key to such a plan would be the nature of the criteria established. I propose the following:

A clear profession of faith in Jesus as the Saviour and Forgiver of one's sins. I do not believe the child needs to describe a dramatic conversion experience, but he should affirm a belief in his or her sinfulness, an understanding of Christ's saving work on the cross, and faith in this work to save him or her from his or her sins.

Knowledge of basic Scriptures such as the Ten Commandments and the Lord's Prayer. All Christians should know these by heart, and other pivotal Scriptures might be added. But the key to acceptance into the body is an understanding of these, marked by the ability to explain their meaning in one's own words.

Knowledge and understanding of the Apostles' Creed. This ancient summary of the faith is a wonderfully concise summary of what a Christian believes. Many churches recite it regularly as an ongoing affirmation of faith. Children in such a church should learn it as a basic 'checklist' of what they believe and in order to participate in that part of the worship service. If a child recites the Creed and affirms his or her belief in it, one must assume that he or she holds to orthodox Christian doctrine and faith.

Mastery, to some degree, of a church catechism, such as *The Westminster Shorter Catechism*. This criterion serves much the same purpose as knowledge of the Apostles' Creed, but gives the child opportunity to express an affirmation of more details about the faith. Since membership in a church should reflect an affirmation of that church's doctrinal tradition, a basic grasp of its teachings should be required.

Demonstration of godly living in seeking to avoid sin and pursue obedience to God. True faith inevitably manifests itself in works (James 2:17). We are not saved by works, but we are not saved if our behaviour doesn't reflect our faith. It is a sensitive matter to evaluate another person's life, but it is dangerous to avoid it altogether in considering individuals for church membership. Children have parents and Sunday-school teachers who should be able to affirm that they show a desire to obey God and sorrow when they fail. They should also show some restraint of sinful tendencies in their words and behaviour. If your church has a mentoring programme, or a specific church leader assigned to the child's family, he or she could be an additional 'character reference'.

Demonstration of an ability to examine oneself so as to discern sin and meet the requirement for properly receiving the Lord's Supper. Questions of whether a child can do this give reason to deny him or her the supper, so demonstration of the ability should give access to the table. When interviewed by church leaders, the child should be able to express an understanding of the meaning of the sacrament and explain what he or she is to do in preparation for it. This should be specifically covered in the interview to protect the child from the consequences of partaking wrongfully.

My hope is that the parents would be with the child for this interview. I also would like to think this was the culmination of preparatory class or a Christian education programme designed to bring children to this point in their lives.

This process would not only serve to prepare children for membership and communion, but play a large part in nurturing them in a faith that would stand against the evils of our day. It would also keep parents and churches focused on the needs of our little ones. Calvin, in commending the 'discipline' of catechizing and examining, cited its benefits:

> If this discipline were in effect today, it would certainly arouse some slothful parents, who carelessly neglect the instruction of their children as a matter of no concern to them; for then they could not overlook it without public disgrace. There would be greater agreement in faith among Christian people, and not so many would go untaught and ignorant; some would not be so rashly carried away with new and strange doctrines; in short, all would have some methodical instruction, so to speak, in Christian doctrine.[2]

Who is in charge of the children?

Those working with children may have a variety of titles: children's director, director of Christian education, minister to children, youth minister, youth director, chair of the children's committee, youth pastor, etc.

What's in a title? A lot, I'd say. Take the difference in the three central words above. A director is someone who gives directions. If I am lost, and swallow my masculine pride to ask for directions, the person will tell me which way to go and what turns to make. They will not get in the car and go with me.

'Minister' is a richer word, suggesting someone who carries out the designs of another on their behalf. In the church, a minister, then, is one who takes the Word of God and the grace of God and brings it to bear on the lives of those in their charge.

A pastor has a rich title also, suggesting he does for his congregation all that a shepherd does for his flock. If we consider only Psalm 23, we see the broad responsibilities it entails, including guidance, protection, provision and companionship.

The importance of these titles was brought home to me several years ago. A pastor once heard me speak on the subject, and shared afterwards that he had realized a mistake. In order to hire a woman to direct his church's children's work (as his church did not believe in the ordination of women), he and the church leadership had altered the title from 'Minister to Children' to 'Children's Director'. He saw that this subtly suggested that the person working with children need not be a genuine minister. In other words, the children did not need someone who was ordained to work with them. They would shift from receiving 'ministry' to receiving 'direction'.

This is a good example of how we can hinder little ones without realizing it. Children are to be ministered to, not merely directed. In fact, they need shepherding as much as any other sheep in the Saviour's flock. They are, after all, the weakest and most vulnerable.

Therefore, I ask you to consider how your church designates the responsibilities for the welfare of children. I submit to you that it should be viewed as a pastoral matter. In smaller churches, the ruling body of the church should oversee the nurture of children. If responsibility is designated, it should be done in a manner consistent with the treatment of adults. In larger churches, those working with children and young people should be designated 'ministers' or 'pastors' and subject to the same ordination require-ments as other pastoral staff. They, of course, may designate some of the work of the ministry to those without such titles, but we need to be clear that our children need shepherding and nothing less.

Similarly, I urge those whom God might call into ministry to consider children's or youth ministry as lifetime callings. All too often these are seen as 'entry level' positions for pastors. I believe that as integral parts of the church, children deserve ministers who are called to work specifically with them and who plan on focusing on that ministry throughout their careers. This would seem a legitimate calling if children are as valuable as we have discovered them to be.

There are doubtlessly other important steps churches can take to care for the smallest members of their flocks more adequately. I pray that these few suggestions will spur you on to find more innovative ways to nurture the children in your church.

13

PRACTICAL STEPS
TOWARDS CHANGE

What we call the beginning is often the end
And to make an end is to make a beginning.
The end is where we start from… (T. S. Eliot)

Congratulations! You have made it to the end. This has not been
the simplest book to read, examining as it does some fairly tough
theological issues. Your persistence to the end betrays a genuine
interest in children and an eagerness to understand their place
in our homes and churches. I would like to help you take the
next step, which is to turn what you have learned into action.
As a warm up, let us summarize briefly the ground we have
covered.

Looking back

Our journey began by our being alerted to the sophisticated ways
in which godless influences impinge on our children's lives. This
is even more alarming given the lack of support for Christian
values found in the culture at large. Our Christian response has
been rather shallow, as many in the church have supped at the

table of relativism and lost commitment to the grand truths of the faith. We saw that God's Word makes it quite clear that children are precious and to be desired. Indeed, they are gifts from God.

Caring for our little ones requires that we properly understand their spiritual nature. Gifts though they are, they are born in original sin. This means they are inclined toward sin and need to be saved. The image of God is grossly distorted, though remnants remain that provide tendencies toward morality and learning. These are drawn upon to teach God's Law and his ways while cautioning children about how these can be used to rationalize selfish ways.

Children, inclined to sin, thus need nurture into the faith. Parents are to provide examples of godly living and create homes where the climate is conducive to the growth of faith, understanding that the seed itself is the gift of God. Even when they profess Christ, children fight the remnants of sin in their lives, and need discipline to learn and practise proper behaviour. We also saw that the responsibility for Christian and academic education falls primarily on the parents as we considered ways to provide these for our children. In summary, we presented the goal of Christian parenting to be to raise children through guidance and discipline to faith in Christ, so that they glorify him in every area of their lives, eventually passing the faith on to their children.

Yet, the church is God's most important institution on earth, and has vital roles to play in the spiritual nurturance of children. Children have always been a part of the covenant community of God's people. As children of believers, they are entitled to baptism as the sign of the covenant. Spiritual understanding and the ability to reflect on the passion of Christ are required for admission to the Lord's Supper. Churches are encouraged to prepare their children for this systematically, and we looked at how they might do it. We reviewed the marvellous evidence in Scripture that God is honoured by the praise of little ones, and so we commend the practice of including children in the worship of the church. We considered some ideas for enhancing the ways our churches might nurture their children.

In brief, we have seen that there is much to be done to care for our children and to protect them from the evils of this world. But where do we start?

Looking ahead

'How many psychologists does it take to change a light bulb?' The answer is 'One, as long as the light bulb really wants to change.' I have found this little ditty helpful in showing my clients that as a psychologist I can provide guidance, but change depends on them. I trust you find yourself wanting to change, so here are some places to begin.

FAMILY CHANGES

We see the urgency of our need to provide careful nurture for our children. Let us look at a few improvements we might make in our homes.

Planning meetings. I hope this book has given you a number of new ideas. But the first step you may want to take is to think through what you are doing now. You and your spouse might write down things you are currently doing to nurture your children in the Lord. (If you have a tough time getting started, go back through Chapters 5–8 and list the qualities of the family that pursues godliness in its children.) Do this separately, and with an eye to comparing your lists at a time when you can be together without the children. See where you agree and disagree. Assess what you are doing well. List areas where you need improvement. Ask yourselves how you might arrange your strategies under our proposed goal for parenting. Consult with your children on this if they are old enough and mature enough. All this should be done in humble and prayerful dependence upon God.

Specify areas that need work. You might identify an area of your life where you believe your example is weak. You might decide to reformulate your discipline plan. You could choose to research your educational options for your children. Then, set up another meeting, with each parent reporting back on his or her topics. By the second meeting, be prepared to state what changes you plan to make in each area. Agree to meet again in a few weeks to hold each other accountable. Some of the changes may be for the individual parent, but others will involve things you want to do as a parental team. Inform the children of what you are doing. You might also join with other parents and have similar meetings in small groups, so long as this does not discourage you from being open about your shortcomings. You will gradually reduce the frequency of such meetings, but they should continue with some frequency, allowing you to monitor your progress and affording structured opportunities for you to pray for your children as a couple. (Though obviously you should pray together often anyway.)

Family worship. In Chapter 5 I outlined the elements for times of family worship. Here I want to encourage you to take specific actions to begin this tradition. I again invite you to read J. W. Alexander's book, *Thoughts on Family Worship*, to increase your excitement about the topic. Then, work out a time for worship that can be kept with some regularity. Most likely this will be in the evenings (if not twice per day).

Remember to include the three major elements of Bible study, prayer and singing. You might begin with something practical like Proverbs, or the gospels if your children are fairly young. With older children, move more into explanations of Scripture. You might need to prepare by studying the passages beforehand. Ask questions to measure what family members learn. Consider how to apply the truths. Your prayer time can begin simply, possibly asking each person to pray for something in particular. Make it inviting and not threatening. Finally, you may wish to designate a musically inclined person to lead in a hymn. If you don't have a hymn book, buy one. Remember, your joyful noise does not have to merit a recording contract!

The most basic thing to bear in mind is to begin with a simple enough 'order of worship' that you can go through it in a meaningful way. The length of time you spend is not as important as its depth. You can easily try to do too much yet accomplish little genuine worship.

Practical godliness. As we made such a point of the importance of the spiritual life of parents, I wish to make particular mention of this here. Your spiritual growth will not be accidental. Seek God's face in the spirit of Psalm 139:23-4 to know areas where you need to change. Study Scripture that applies to these areas, and read good Christian books on the topics. (Remember that old books have much to offer. The Puritans in particular had a lot to say about practical godliness, especially in relation to family life.)

You may seek the counsel of a mentor for yourself. It might be an elder in your church or another person you esteem in the faith. If not, then consider meeting regularly with a friend. Hold each other accountable for problem spots you are working on.

B ehaviour management. Just a reminder here of the importance of dealing with children's behaviour fairly and without exasperating them. This should almost always be a topic in your parental meetings. Agree on which behaviour will meet with which consequences. Like the laws of the community, the consequences children face for their 'misdemeanours' should not vary with the 'police officer' on duty. If a child does something wrong, the punishment should be the same whether mum or dad is on duty.

Consequences vary from child to child and age to age. Even if you develop a very effective plan for discipline, don't become complacent. As your children grow, you will have to make changes. Be committed to the process, not just the plan.

E ducation. If you have not given your children's schooling as much thought as you think you should, make it a topic for a parental summit or two. Then, once you are comfortable with your choice (be it public, private, or home school), re-evaluate it annually for each child. As we noted earlier, there is not a 'one size fits all' position on education.

C hurch involvement. I have sought to stress the importance of the church in the life of families. Yet, churches cannot provide effective ministries without having opportunity. I firmly believe that all believers should be strongly committed to a local church. Are you? If not, seek God's guidance about where you should commit yourselves. If you are, evaluate your involvement. How else might you participate? Are your children benefiting as they should? For some families, this will mean they need to be less involved.

CHANGES IN OUR CHURCHES

One of my prayers for this book is that it will increase awareness among pastors and other church leaders of the indispensable ministry that we have to our children. Many will have theological differences with some of my conclusions, but I trust all will agree that we must be very aggressive in nurturing the little ones in our midst. For those in church leadership, and others who might approach their leadership with some ideas, I offer some inaugural steps to a more comprehensive ministry to children.

A philosophy of ministry. To be accredited colleges have to state their purpose and goals clearly. This is because accrediting agencies know good education doesn't happen haphazardly. Similarly, churches will be more effective in the training of their children if they have a stated 'philosophy of ministry to children'.

Such a statement would include the church's beliefs about the nature of children, their spiritual needs, their place within the structure of the church, and the church's responsibilities to them and their families. It would present the church's position on infant baptism, the admission of children to membership and Communion, and the place of children in corporate worship.

The ruling body of the church might appoint a committee to study these matters and draw up a draft for others in the church to review. They could consult any documents available within their denomination or tradition, and also survey parents and children as to their impressions of strengths and weaknesses of the church's ministry to children and youth.

Such a statement could lead to specific goals for the ministry that in turn would specify the changes needed to pursue those goals. For example, if the goal was for all children to be taught a catechism, then the leadership could spell out when it would be taught and by whom. It should establish a way in which responsibilities for programmes are determined and decisions approved.

Once such a philosophy of ministry was in place, the leadership could determine how best to educate the congregation about it. A central aspect of nurturing the children of a church is that the parents and body as a whole grasp the nature of what they believe about children. The entire church needs to be aware of what they offer to help parents raise children in the faith. An annual sermon on children would be beneficial, possibly on a children's emphasis Sunday where adult Sunday-school lessons would cover the biblical teachings about the value of children or their place in the body of Christ.

M entoring programmes. Church leaders are encouraged prayerfully to consider providing mentors to families, children, and/or young people. It might be best to target a specific group to start, and to find out how many suitable mentors would be willing to participate. To be meaningful, a mentoring programme need not be comprehensive. This added support and guidance could prove most influential in the lives of even a few children. This might be most useful for families who seek the church's help in difficult circumstances (such as single parents, rebellious teens, financial hardship, or new believers).

C hristian education. Most churches designate someone to plan the curriculum for Sunday-school. If criteria for admission into the membership of the church were stated in the philosophy of ministry, these would greatly assist this planner in his or her task. As noted earlier, the curriculum should be designed with a long-term view, not just year by year. As our schools build each year on what was taught the one before, so should our churches.

Additionally, other educational programmes could be designed to help parents with their children. Many churches offer parenting classes, and their frequent focus on behaviour management is important. But seminars might also be offered on how to use a catechism, beginning family worship, ways to teach children compassion, or how to be a critical media consumer.

It is hoped that the leadership of the church would endeavour to keep the significance of children before the congregation and encourage the congregation and its individual families in nurturing.

Prayer. The ruling body of the church might consider leading the congregation in a day of prayer for the children of the church and the community. They might appoint someone to begin a regular time of prayer for children. Prayer lists for times of assembly for general prayer might include specific ways to pray for the little ones of the church, their families, and those who minister to them.

Leadership. As it is ultimately the pastor and other leadership of the church that bear responsibility for the health and safety of the flock, they should consider supervision of ministry to children as part of their jobs. They should learn the names of the children (church photo directories are very helpful here), and systematically pray for them. They might assign each family to a church leader who would let the family know they are under his care. He will pray for them and monitor their spiritual health, encouraging family worship and catechizing while being accessible in times of need and celebration.

Outreach. Finally, since all children are God's gifts, and given the example of Jesus, we should reach out to the children around us. Children are a fertile field for evangelism, and terribly vulnerable to their environments. Churches should initiate and support ministries to homeless children, chronically ill children, and poor children. We should lead the way in providing adoptive families and foster homes for displaced children. Churches might offer free tutoring for children struggling in school or who are educationally disadvantaged. This is all part of loving our neighbour as ourselves.

Church leaders might choose a particular area for outreach to children in the community, put it into the church budget, and designate leadership to get adults and children within the church involved.

But the community does not stop at the city line. In our missions conferences, we should always draw attention to some form of ministry to children in other countries. Encourage families to adopt hungry children through Christian relief agencies, or to support those who minister to children. Sunday school classes might commit themselves to praying for the children of a particular missionary family. While we often pray for the work of the parents, we are prone to neglect the hardships missionary children endure for the sake of the gospel. Such personal approaches can touch the heart of compassion in many of our children.

I have listed quite a number of opportunities for churches to become more explicit in their ministry to children. I exhort the leaders of churches to consider which ones fit the needs of their congregations and then get started. The need is great and the rewards are eternal.

For the faint of heart

You may look at this long list of suggestions and be overwhelmed. There seems to be so much to be done and you may feel you lack the energy or initiative to be the parent or leader you should be. I recall the motto on a colleague's coffee mug: 'Progress, not perfection.' This is a wise admonition. Feeling we cannot minister to children perfectly may discourage us from taking initial steps. This reminds us of the old Chinese proverb, 'The journey of a thousand miles begins with a single step.'

I hope you journey far in your ministry to your children, but for now I encourage you to take the first step. One change in your family will make a difference in the lives of your children. One person in your church praying for children and promoting their needs can further God's kingdom in many ways. For we remember the words with which Christ comforted the apostle Paul, 'My grace is sufficient for you, for my power is made perfect in weakness' (2 Cor. 12:9).

The end is the beginning

I was confused in high school. I couldn't figure out why the graduation was called 'commencement'. To 'commence' something is to begin it, right? I thought we were finishing something, and then they tried to call it a beginning.

Well, I may be slow, but I caught on. They call it 'commencement' because, upon finishing high school, you are no longer a child and you are ready to 'commence' your adult life and to use the things you learned in school. That's the catch: the end is just the beginning. T. S. Eliot expresses the idea well in the quotation which opened this chapter.

I hope this book serves to 'commence' your nurturance of your children and those of others in new and vital ways. We have covered some rough territory. Doctrines like original sin and infant baptism are formidable. I admit the applications of Scripture to issues about children are challenging, and I don't want to leave the impression that I have the last word on these matters. I say with Paul, 'Oh, the depth of the riches of the wisdom and knowledge of God! How unsearchable his judgments, and his paths beyond tracing out' (Rom. 11:33).

Yet, our children are too important to avoid these matters. We must seek God's direction in our understanding, and take action on his Word. Our children are growing every moment, and will be grown sooner than we imagine. He has honoured us with the title of 'parents', or with the privilege of ministering our spiritual gifts in the lives of others. We must respond with vigorous obedience, and with the joy of knowing we please God as we serve the little ones.

Children bring us great joy and great anxiety. They delight us and frustrate us. Loving them means leading them in the ways of God, for their greatest pleasure will be found in pleasing him. May our gracious heavenly Father, who by great sacrifice made us his sons and daughters, grant us wisdom and grace so that we do not hinder our children, for 'of such is the kingdom of God'.

> O God, I cannot endure to see the
>   destruction of my kindred.
> Let those that are united to me in tender ties
>   be precious in thy sight
>   and devoted to thy glory.
> Sanctify and prosper my domestic devotion,
>   instruction, discipline, example,
>   that my house may be a nursery for heaven,
>   my church the garden of the Lord,
>   enriched with the trees of righteousness of
>   thy planting, for thy glory;
> Let not those of my family who are amiable,
>   moral, attractive, fall short of heaven at last;
> Grant that the promising appearances of

tender conscience, soft heart,
the alarms and delights of the Word,
be not finally blotted out,
but bring forth judgment unto victory in all
whom I love.[1]

Soli Deo Gloria!

NOTES

Chapter 1: Christian Parenting in a Hostile World

[1] Charles Colson citing George Barna, 'The Year of the Neopagan', *Christianity Today*, March 6, 1995.

[2] Quoted in Gene Edward Veith, Jr., *Postmodern Times: A Christian Guide to Contemporary Thought and Culture* (Wheaton, IL: Crossway Books, 1994), p. 75.

[3] *Ibid*, p. 75.

[4] John Sommerville, *The Discovery of Childhood in Puritan England* (Athens, GA: University of Georgia Press, 1992), p. 25.

Chapter 2: Blessings, Not Burdens

[1] John Calvin on Psalm 127 in his *Commentary on the Book of Psalms*, in *Calvin's Commentaries*, 22 vols. (Grand Rapids, MI: Baker, 1984), vol. 6.

[2] C. H. Spurgeon on Psalm 127:3 in *The Treasury of David* (McLean, VA: MacDonald, n.d.).

[3] Calvin, *op. cit.*

[4] Justin Martyr, *The First Apology of Justin*, ch. xxvii, in Philip Schaff (ed), *The Ante-Nicene Fathers* (Grand Rapids, MI: Eerdmans, 1985), vol. 1, p. 173.

[5] Tertullian, *Apology*, ch. ix. in Philip Schaff (ed), *The Ante-Nicene Fathers* (Grand Rapids, MI: Eerdmans, 1986), vol. 3, p. 25.

Chapter 3: Innocents or Devils?

1. G. C. Berkouwer, *Man: The Image of God*, in *Studies in Dogmatics* (Grand Rapids, MI: Eerdmans, 1962), vol. 8, p. 72.
2. John Calvin, *Institutes of the Christian Religion* (1559), ed. John T. McNeill (Philadelphia: Westminster Press, 1960), I. xv. 3.
3. Augustine, *The City of God*, bk. XII, ch. 23, in Philip Schaff (ed), *The Nicene and Post-Nicene Fathers* (Grand Rapids, MI: Eerdmans, 1983), p. 241.
4. *The Westminster Confession of Faith* (1646) (Scotland: Free Press Publications, 1981), Chapter IV, Section 2.
5. Calvin, *Institutes*, I. xv. 3.
6. Carl F. H. Henry, *God Who Speaks and Shows*, in *God, Revelation, and Authority*. 6 vols. (Waco. TX: Word, 1976), vol. 1, p. 76.
7. Geoffrey Bromiley, 'Concupiscence', in Everett F. Harrison (ed), *Dictionary of New Testament Theology* (Grand Rapids, MI: Baker, 1960), pp. 64–65.

Chapter 4: How and When Can Children Be Saved?

1. R. A. Webb, *The Theology of Infant Salvation* (1907) (Harrisonburg, VA: Sprinkle, 1991), p.180.
2. Geoffrey Bromiley, *Children of Promise: The Case for Baptizing Infants* (Grand Rapids, MI: Eerdmans, 1979), p. 99.
3. C. H. Spurgeon, *Come Ye Children, A Book for Parents and Teachers on the Christian Training of Children* (Pasadena, TX: Pilgrim, n.d), p.36.
4. John Calvin, *Institutes of the Christian Religion*, III.xxi.7.
5. This summary is based on Chapter VII of *The Westminster Confession of Faith* (1646), which offers a helpful summary of the covenants. For a more in-depth discussion of covenant theology, see Louis Berkof, *Manual of Christian Doctrine* (Grand Rapids, MI: Eerdmans, 1933), pp. 130–171, and A. A. Hodge, *Outlines of Theology* (1879) (Grand Rapids, MI: Zondervan, 1973), pp. 309–314, 367–377.
6. I am grateful to Edward N. Gross for summarizing these texts in his book, *Will My Children Go to Heaven? Hope and Help for Believing Parents* (Phillipsburg, NJ: P&R Publishing, 1995), chapters 3–4.
7. John Calvin on Matthew 19:14 in *Calvin's Commentaries*, Vol. XVI, p. 390.
8. James Janeway & Cotton Mather, *A Token for Children* (Pittsburgh: Soli Deo Gloria, 1994), pp. 22–25.

Chapter 5: Cultivating Godly Children: What's a Parent to Do?

1 R. S. Anderson, 'The family as matrix of character', in *Theology News and Notes*, Vol. 35, 3, p. 24.
2 John Calvin, *Commentaries on the Epistles of Paul to the Galatians and Ephesians*, in *Calvin's Commentaries*, vol. XXI, p. 317.
3 Matthew Henry, A *Commentary on the Whole Bible*. 6 vols. (Old Tappan, NJ: Fleming H. Revell, n.d.), vol. VI., p. 715.
4 Calvin, *op. cit.*, p. 329.
5 *Ibid.*
6 J. Behm, 'Noeo', in Geoffrey W. Bromiley, (ed.), *Theological Dictionary of the New Testament*, (Grand Rapids, MI: Eerdmans, abridged edn. 1985), pp. 636–646.
7 Originally published 1847. Reprinted by Soli Deo Gloria Publications, 1994.

Chapter 6: The School of Life—Parents are Teachers

1 Jerry Bridges, *The Joy of Fearing God* (Colorado Springs: Waterbrook Press, 1998), p. 18.
2 I borrow this term from David Wells' profound book, *God in the Wasteland: The Reality of Truth in a World of Fading Dreams* (Grand Rapids, M: Eerdmans 1994).
3 This practice is related in detail in the classic work of Richard Baxter, *The Reformed Pastor* (1656) (Edinburgh: Banner of Truth, 1974).

Chapter 7: Disciplining Disciples

1 Matthew Henry, on Proverbs 22:15, A *Commentary on the Whole Bible*, 6 vols. (Old Tappan, NJ: Fleming H. Revell, n.d.).

Chapter 8: Teaching Children to Honour Their Parents

1 John Calvin, *Institutes of the Christian Religion*, II. viii. 35–38.

Chapter 9: Where Do Children Fit in the Church?

1 Rodney Clapp, *Families at the Crossroads: Beyond Traditional and Modern Options* (Downer's Grove, IL: InterVarsity Press, 1994), pp. 76–78.
2 William Hendriksen, *The Gospel of Matthew* (Grand Rapids: Baker, 1973), p. 687.
3 *Ibid* on Matthew 18:10.

4 Matthew Henry, on Matthew 18:10, in *A Commentary on the Whole Bible* V: 255.

5 John Calvin, *Harmony of the Evangelists*, 2:338 in *Calvin's Commentaries*, vol. XVI.

6 C. H. Spurgeon, *Come Ye Children* (Pasadena, TX: Pilgrim Publications, n.d.), p. 35.

7 Calvin, *op. cit.*, 2:390.

8 Charles Hodge, *Systematic Theology*. 3 vols. (Grand Rapids: Eerdmans, reprinted 1981), vol. 3, p. 552.

9 G. Campbell Morgan, *The Westminster Pulpit: The Preaching of G. Campbell Morgan*. 10 vols. (Originally published by Hodder and Stoughton, 1906–1909; reprinted Grand Rapids, MI: Baker, n.d.), III: 68.

Chapter 10: Children and the Sacraments

1 The interested reader is referred to the sources cited in this chapter for additional information on the subject. The books by Bromiley and Murray are especially helpful. A rather different approach is found in the fascinating work by James M. Chaney, *William the Baptist* (1877) (Recently reissued by the Reformed Presbyterian Church Evangelical Synod, n.d.). You might also wish to review books from your tradition if it is different. Your pastor should prove helpful in directing you to appropriate sources.

2 David. L. Neilands, *Studies in the Covenant of Grace* (Phillipsburg, NJ: Presbyterian and Reformed, 1980), p. 60.

3 John Calvin, *Institutes of the Christian Religion*, IV. xvi. 20.

4 Neilands, *op. cit.*, p. 89.

5 John Calvin, in *Calvin's Commentaries*, Vol. XX, *ad. loc.*

6 John Murray, *Christian Baptism* (Phillipsburg, NJ: Presbyterian and Reformed, 1980), p. 65.

7 *Ibid.*, p. 83.

8 Calvin, *Institutes*, IV. xvi. 17.

9 Neilands, *op. cit.*, p. 166.

10 *The Westminster Confession of Faith*, ch. XXV, sec. II.

11 Calvin, *Institutes*, IV. xvi. 9.

12 G. R. Beasley-Murray, 'The Child and the Church', in Clifford Ingle, (Ed.), *Children and Conversion* (Nashville, TN: Broadman, 1970), p. 132.

13 Calvin, *Institutes*, IV. xvi. 19.

14 Murray, *op. cit.*, p. 153.

15 *Ibid.*, p. 77.

16 Calvin, *Institutes*, IV. xvi. 15.

17 John Calvin, *Commentary on the Epistles of Paul to the Corinthians*, in *Calvin's Commentaries* Vol. XX, *ad. loc.*

18 *Ibid.*, ad. loc.

Chapter 11: From the Mouths of Babes

1. C. H. Spurgeon, *The Treasury of David*, 3 vols. (McLean, VA: Macdonald, n.d.), Vol. I., p.80.
2. John Calvin, *Calvin's Commentaries* Vol. IV, *ad. loc.*
3. Richard Bacon, *Revealed to Babes: Children in the Worship of God* (Audubon, NJ: Old Paths, 1993), p. 27.
4. *Ibid.*, p. 58.
5. *Ibid.*
6. In *Trinity Hymnal* (Philadelphia: Great Commission Publications, 1961), Hymn no. 117, verses 1 and 5.

Chapter 12: The Spiritual Nurture of Children in the Church

1. John Calvin, *Institutes of the Christian Religion*, IV. xix. 13.
2. *Ibid.*

Chapter 13: Practical Steps Towards Change

1. From 'The Family' in Arthur Bennett (ed.) *The Valley of Vision: A Collection of Puritan Prayers & Devotions* (Edinburgh: Banner of Truth, 1975), p.113.

WORLD-PROOF YOUR KIDS

RAISING CHILDREN UNSTAINED
BY THE WORLD

TIM SISEMORE

WITH RUTH SISEMORE

World-proof Your Kids:

Raising Children Unstained by the World

Tim Sisemore with Ruth Sisemore

Many Christian parents are at their wits end about raising their children in a healthy and spiritual way. Increasingly the influence of the world, with it's 'me first' obsession, is causing problems within the Christian home.

This influence causes Christian families to fall into the four categories:

- The disillusioned family
- The distracted family
- The disciplinarian family
- The dedicated family

All end up being influenced by the culture rather than by their faith.

Is your family influenced by the culture rather than your faith. Is your family falling into an unhealthy pattern of behaviour? It's time to find out and put things right.

If you want to help your family then the Sisemore's are here to help break the cycle.

ISBN 978-1-84550-275-1

HOMEWARD
BOUND

Building an attractive
Christ-centered family
on eternal principles

EDWARD A. HARTMAN

Homeward Bound:

Building an Attractive Christ-centred Family on Eternal Principles

Edward A. Hartman

We live in a consumer culture that exalts and commends living with a passion for the moment – our society depends on it. We have bought a subtle lie that there will be no day of final accounting – and so our children don't live with an eternal perspective.

When Ed's wife, Amy, died from that brain tumor, all the flowers at the funeral did not come with a card saying 'with our condolences' but with the phrase *'welcome to your new home'* – a phrase Amy picked out herself. As Ed says:

"Few things, like death, will put life in perspective. And few things, like accountability, will put obedience in perspective. This life is transitional; it can prepare us to be welcomed into our new, eternal home. And it provides us with a lifetime of opportunities to invite others along, beginning with our own families."

So join in with Ed and his family as they explore what makes a Godly home – and a way of attractively displaying and persuasively commending the glory of God in the life of a Christian family.

'For the Christian, the best is always yet to be. Ed Hartman reminds us of this in a way that comforts, challenges and inspires... I commend it warmly.'

Alistair Begg,
Senior Pastor, Parkside Church, Chagrin Falls, Ohio

'If your heart thirsts not for pious platitudes from the complacent but for real comfort from a brother who has found God faithful in the valley of death's shadow, read this book.'

Dennis E. Johnson,
Professor of Practical Theology, Westminster Seminary, Escondido, California

Edward A. Hartman and his wife, Emily are currently missionaries with Mission to the World (PCA) in Romania. Prior to that Edward was the senior pastor of First Presbyterian Church (PCA) in Kosciusko, Mississippi.

ISBN 978-1-84550-348-2

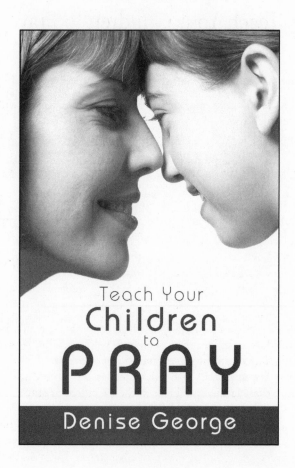

Teach Your
Children
to
PRAY

Denise George

Teach Your Children to Pray

Denise George

In a nut-shell this book is a non judgmental, practical, hands-on, I've been there approach to Christian parenting... with a wonderful, inspiring, get me started focus on prayer. Yet it doesn't compromise on the truth and the challenge of God's word. Once you start reading it you will realise the value of prayer, you will be itching to start it with your child, you will learn and your family will learn the importance of communicating with God.

Denise George, is a mother, Christian and human being. Her book is written on the back of a life time of experience, mistakes, triumphs, problems, ideas, inspiration, questions, scripture reading... and prayer.

Read this book to be challenged by the call to teach your child to pray. You'll be encouraged by the honest "I've been there," approach of the author. You're going to be inspired by the wonderful activities and ideas sections. And those really difficult questions that you've wanted to ask someone but haven't dared – have a look at the question section. There's probably someone who has asked that question before you.

Every family should read this. Every family should use this. Because every family should teach their children to pray!

A prolific and inspirational writer Denise George is well known for writing books that are creative and biblical. Her husband Timothy is the executive editor of Christianity Today and is the founding dean of Beeson Divinity school.

IBSN 978-1-85792-941-6

IT'S OK TO CRY

CRY FINDING HOPE WHEN STRUGGLING WITH **INFERTILITY** & **MISCARRIAGE**

'This book will be deeply treasured.' **R. T. Kendall**

MALCOLM & NICK CAMERON

It's Ok to Cry

Finding hope when struggling with inferility and miscarriage

Malcolm & Nick Cameron

Many couples live with the ache of not being able to have children. Malcolm and Nick Cameron are writing from such a background themselves. This book tells of their struggles as they coped with years of infertility and will take you through the story of their miscarriage and the task of piecing their lives back to together afterwards. Throughout their ups and downs, and amidst the heartache, Malcolm and Nick have been carried through by God, and emerged on the other side stronger than before. This book will help you whether you are going through a similar situation or if you have a friend or family member that is facing the heartache of longing for, or losing, a baby.

"Obviously a book like this will contain a great deal of talk about feelings and emotions, but Malcolm and Nick always come back to God's Word and his faithfulnessas their anchor point..I found the book a compelling read...Thank you Malcolm and Nick, for not pretending to that you've got it it all figured out. or that it never hurts anyone. IT'S OK TO CRY is a reminder that God's goodness and faithfulness does not depend on us getting what we want."

Janet Gaukroger,

This book is not for the faint-hearted. It's written for those who are suffering the intense pain of bereavement in childlessness. It's raw, real and compulsory reading for those who want to enter in and understand something of the pain some childless couples are called to endure. Sometimes God miraculously answers prayers for a child, but the complete answer hasn't come yet for Malcolm and Nick. It's OK to Cry is about a couple who experience the untold heartache of not seeing their desires realized and who live to tell the tale, and rejoice in the Lord.

Lyndon Bowring, CARE

ISBN 978-1-84550-077-1

Christian Focus Publications
publishes books for all ages

Our mission statement –

STAYING FAITHFUL
In dependence upon God we seek to help make His infallible Word, the Bible, relevant. Our aim is to ensure that the Lord Jesus Christ is presented as the only hope to obtain forgiveness of sin, live a useful life and look forward to heaven with Him.

REACHING OUT
Christ's last command requires us to reach out to our world with His gospel. We seek to help fulfil that by publishing books that point people towards Jesus and help them develop a Christ-like maturity. We aim to equip all levels of readers for life, work, ministry and mission.

Books in our adult range are published in three imprints.

Christian Focus contains popular works including biographies, commentaries, basic doctrine and Christian living. Our children's books are also published in this imprint.

Mentor focuses on books written at a level suitable for Bible College and seminary students, pastors, and other serious readers. The imprint includes commentaries, doctrinal studies, examination of current issues and church history.

Christian Heritage contains classic writings from the past.

Christian Focus Publications Ltd
Geanies House, Fearn,
Ross-shire, IV20 1TW, Scotland, United Kingdom
info@christianfocus.com

Our titles are available from quality bookstores and
www.christianfocus.com